To Ian   Happy.

G000243183

My Kind of Rugby

My Kind of Rugby
Union and League

Ray French

Faber & Faber
London   Boston

First published in 1979
by Faber and Faber Limited
3 Queen Square London WC1N 3AU
Printed in Great Britain by
Redwood Burn Limited Trowbridge and Esher
All rights reserved
© Ray French 1979

British Library Cataloguing in Publication Data

French, Ray
  My kind of rugby
  1. Rugby football
  I. Title
  796.33'32   GV945
  ISBN 0 571 11422 9

CONTENTS

ILLUSTRATIONS

9 England v Scotland, Twickenham, March 1961. A tussle for a loose ball following a line-out. Ray French, in scrum cap, appears to be wrestling with C.R. Jacobs, England's No. 1.

10 Chaired by his team-mates, Vince Karalius, the St. Helens captain, holds the Lancashire Cup after his side had defeated Swinton in the 1962 Final.

11 St. Helens v New Zealand, Knowsley Road, St. Helens, 1961. The determination is there, but French suffers a heavy tackle as he tries to break out of defence.

12 A training-session shortly after French's signing for St. Helens in August 1961. Coach Stan McCormick explains the finer points of forward play to (*l. to r.*) Mike Knowles, Cliff Watson, Ray French and Keith Ashcroft.

13 A triumphant dive by Ray French as he scores the winning try a couple of minutes before full-time in the Western Championship Final against Swinton at Central Park, Wigan, 1964.

14 With the ball tucked firmly under his arm, French makes a determined run at the Hull K.R. defence in the semi-final of the 1966 Championship play-off.

15 Tommy Bishop, confidently perching on Ray French's shoulder, uses a ball to demonstrate how he will hold the cup aloft in a break from training during the build-up to the 1966 Wembley Cup Final.

16 Under the watchful eye of Ray French, Prime Minister Harold Wilson is introduced to John Mantle before the start of the Rugby League Cup Final between St. Helens and Wigan in 1966.

17 Although there is no love lost between two sides during a final, French still has time for a smile after a duel with Wigan's skipper Eric Ashton.

18 With a blessing from a supporter, Alec Murphy, the St. Helens captain, leads his smiling, victorious team back to the pitch after receiving the Rugby League Challenge Cup from Prime Minister Harold Wilson in 1966.

19 Victory is sweet. Murphy holds the cup aloft to show the St. Helens supporters, while delighted team-mates look to find wives, relatives and friends in the crowd.

20 The Great Britain Rugby League side before playing France at the Parc des Princes, Paris, 1968.
Back row: I. Brooke, C. Renilson, M. Clarke, C. Watson, A. Morgan, R. French, J. Warlow, K. Edwards. *Front row:* B. Risman, F. Flanagan, C. Young, R. Millward, N. Fox, T. Bishop, A. Burwell.

21 England v France, Bradford, 1968. Ray French and Ian Brooke look on as Chris Young is firmly tackled.

22 Ray French, seen off for Australia at the airport by his wife in 1968, signs an autograph for the daughter of the Widnes physiotherapist Frank Tobin.

23 Great Britain v Australia, Sydney Cricket Ground, 1968. Cliff Watson, supported by Ray French, drives for the line.

24 The Great Britain tour party in the airport coach on the way from Sydney to Brisbane for the match against Queensland, July 1968. Front seats occupied by (*l. to r.*) Arnie Morgan (Featherstone Rvrs.), Mick Clarke (Leeds), Chris Young (Hull K.R.) and Clive Sullivan (Hull). Tommy Bishop (St. Helens) (seated behind Chris Young) reads a press report. Ray French is seated behind Bishop.

25 Ray French caught in a characteristic pose on the touch-line in a photograph taken by a pupil at Cowley School. (All the action is off camera.)

26 French demonstrates the importance of keeping the eye on the ball as he is put under pressure by one of his young players.

27 French's students listen intently as he explains a point on scrummaging.

28 Teaching boys the basic rugby skills is vital to the game's future. Here French receives a well-delivered pass.

29 The other Ray French in teaching attire at Cowley School.

Acknowledgements

The author is grateful to the following for permission to reproduce photographs in which they hold the copyright: Sport and General Press Agency (plates 1–9); Geoff Williams (plates 10, 13–16, 18, 19, 29) and Jack Hicks (plate 21).

Foreword

by

DICK JEEPS

Chairman of the Sports Council

Ray French, of St. Helens, played for England under my captaincy in 1960/61 and knew as much about simple, direct forward tactics as anyone I have known—and he was a great team man.

Ray disliked unnecessary mauling and rough play as much as I did, and this in itself guarantees a book that may go a long way in correcting the modern trend towards over-complicated systems and, unfortunately, sheer brutality in the pack.

What is also very important is that Ray has been coaching schoolboys for the past eighteen years. With his deep knowledge of both Rugby Union and Rugby League, and his experience in getting vital points across to youngsters, he is just the fellow to bring on a new generation of rugby players who should imbue this great game of ours with fresh courage, inspiration and straight thinking.

R.E.G.J.

Preface

by

MIKE STEVENSON

Northern Rugby correspondent, Daily and Sunday Telegraph

Ray French, one of the most distinguished rugby men in the country, is among my favourite sportsmen.

In an age when so many sporting gladiators are arrogantly self-centred or obsessed with greed, he genuinely prefers to keep what it has become fashionable to describe as a low profile—that is apart from his flat cap. Ray's own personal emblem, as instantly recognizable as Churchill's cigar, is even visible in a photograph I possess of the great man coaching his beloved Cowley School XV in immaculate rugby kit plus flat cap.

Talk to the Cowley boys who have played in Ray's teams over the years and a combination of respect and affectionate amusement will at once be apparent. I recently asked Steve Tickle, the former Waterloo captain, now playing Rugby League for Barrow, at what stage he realized that in Mike Burke Waterloo possessed a potential star. Back came the deadpan answer: 'Oh, years ago when Frenchy told us he was a good 'un.'

Yet the flood of class players that Ray has coached to distinction over the years will testify that they have been taught to lose graciously as well as win, for Ray French is not just a rugby man by a dedicated schoolmaster who really cares for the young people in his charge. But although the most friendly and approachable of men, he does not appreciate company on the touch-line when Cowley are playing. You will usually see him near one of the dead-ball lines in dignified isolation, recalling the statue in Don Giovanni—apart from the flat cap!

It is a lucky man who is both contented with his home and happy in his work. Such a man is Ray French. More important than the games he played for England and Great Britain is the man himself, his attitude to life, to young people and to the great game that has influenced him and that he has influenced.

M.H.S.

Author's Preface

Being an avid reader and a well-established fireside critic of rugby books, I have long wanted to add my own thoughts to the material available. I have enjoyed the biographies of great players in both Rugby Union and Rugby League who rose from obscurity to fame, and have scoured with interest the accounts of touring sides both at home and abroad, often looking for coaching hints and techniques which I could pass on to my team. However, I have rarely found the book which allows a reader to look at both codes together. So from the unique position of having been an international player at both League and Union, with experience of coaching at club and schoolboy levels in both games, I hope to be able to open a window on the relationship between them.

Though my career has formed the basis of the narrative, I hope that I have kept it sufficiently wide-ranging so as to avoid this being the 'Ray French Story'. Nor have I sought to select another endless supply of World XVs or XIIIs. Instead I have endeavoured to assess the strengths and weaknesses of the two games; and as I enjoy both Union and League I feel free of any bias to one or the other. Consequently I hope my opinions and judgements will arouse some debate; so too may my ideas of future trends.

As well as providing food for thought for the adherents of League or Union, I hope that I can provide both them and the less committed with an insight into the workings, characters, and atmosphere of rugby. By entering the world of the dressing-rooms, the field of play and the training nights, I have aimed to reveal the aspirations, attitudes, and emotions which are common or contrasting within the two games.

Throughout my career I have gained tremendous enjoyment and incentive from working alongside players of the highest class and have obtained the greatest rewards in encouraging the club and schoolboy player to fulfil his potential. And from all of them I have enjoyed a rich vein of humour.

Above all, I hope to illustrate that whatever differences may occur, whatever attitudes may exist, the love for an oval ball has few demarcation lines. Though there is a wide gulf between the administration and hence the outlook in the management of both codes, there is an area common to players, coaches, spectators and schoolboys which, because of the pressures within the codes, is bringing them closer together.

1
Born to Rugby

'Room for four more on top', the shrill, piercing shout of the young but perky conductress rose above the smoke and crispness of the cold on that Boxing Day afternoon as we jostled each other in the dash for seats on the top deck of the one o'clock Saints Special bus. It was St. Helens v Wigan—Rugby League's answer to the Roman Games. A sea of flat caps, hardly out of their Christmas wrappers, trilbies, and buttoned overcoats could not hide the smiling and contented faces of the miners and glass-workers on their way to the peak of everyone's Christmas—the match! With red and white scarves wrapped around their necks, only the faces could be seen as all chatted eagerly of the prospects of the local side. This was to be Wigan's come-uppance.

'Gullick will bloody murder him', could be heard from a most knowledgeable pensioner, sitting on the back seat, and we lads all nodded in silent agreement. Jokes and ribald comment were passed to and fro as the young girl attempted to take the fares while sipping a nip of rum from one of the many hip-flasks held in reserve for the ceremony of drinks and turkey sandwiches among workmates at half-time. After what seemed an age, we were deposited outside the ground in Knowsley Road to be met by yet another tide of red and white scarves making its way past the unending bales of straw removed from the frost-bitten pitch that very morning. With the smells of straw, rum, and fish from the local fish and chip shop, we all knew it was Boxing Day again. Lads of all shapes and sizes left dad to join the queue for the boy's pen, a caged area which was reminiscent of Colditz, reserved exclusively for the kids at ninepence. Older ones bent low at the turnstile in their time-honoured dodge of getting round the gateman— 'I'm only thirteen mister, honest.' This was the pen where players were hero-worshipped and where countless fights were started over the right to return the ball after some

1

attempt at goal. Many an international player has waited those countless minutes until a winner emerged to return the ball with an effort.

The details and intricacies were above our heads as we tried to follow the cut and thrust of this local derby with the roars and groans from the 30,000 rabid fans. But somehow we were part of it, both the scene and the atmosphere, all worshipping at the font of the Saints. Our heroes were men such as Don Gullick, a Welshman of huge, craggy proportions whose build indicated a second-row forward but who played at centre-threequarter and whose frame would have removed the dressing-room door if it had stood in the way of a try. Truly a gentle giant off the field, Gullick was sheer strength on it. He was partnered by Duggie Greenall, an international centre of barely eleven stones, but a player who was to strike fear into the hearts of the Australians when he visited them on tour. Reputed by the Aussies to wear sticking plaster on his elbows, he was feared for his tackle, known as the 'mammy', in which after a flying leap he wrapped himself round his opponent and invariably left him for dead on the floor. 'Give 'em mammy, Duggie' was the crowd's constant cry. The game was hard in the early fifties, but it still had its finesse in the shape of men like Stan McCormick, the club's side-stepping winger and master of the interception try. He had set Rugby League alight in 1948 by his then world-record transfer fee of £4,000, when he was signed by St. Helens from the now extinct Belle Vue Rangers in Manchester. These men filled us with excitement during the match and with dreams on our way home as we picked sides for the accustomed game of 'tick' rugby in the park. With coats on the ground for goal posts, we divided into two teams and when a player carrying the ball was touched by a would-be tackler the ball was given to the other side— 'I'm Gullick.' 'No you're not. I'm Gullick, you're Ashton.' 'I'm captain then.'

We were an integral part of the town's rugby then just as much as I was to be some fifteen years later on a similar cold day in 1966, sitting in the crowded dresssing-room drinking the ever-faithful bottle of shandy and looking at the stained faces of the players as they trooped in after the game. With the effects of a pain-killing injection in my back (hurriedly inserted at half-time) now beginning to wear off, and a cauliflower ear just beginning to sprout, I asked myself, 'Why play this game?' On seeing Frankie Barrow, our full-back, I was answered. Despite his gashed eyebrow and blood streaming down the side of his head, he was still smiling broadly at scoring the vital try in our 8–3 win over Wigan—the reason was pride! Wigan, in the shape of Eric Ashton, Chris Hesketh and Terry Fogerty, had displayed all the skills of rugby in the second-half. We had covered many miles across the field in defence during the last twenty minutes, holding out against their fierce attack. We had even managed to stifle the menace of the renowned Billy Boston, the Welsh wing from Cardiff, who, although he had the skill to beat his opponents with a sidestep or a swerve, always seemed to enjoy using his fifteen stones to smash them to the ground. My knees had been scraped raw on the ice-rutted pitch not just for the £40 pay packet at the end of the week or the one-line quotation from Jack Bentley in the *Daily Express*, 'French did the grafting and tackling of two men', but because it was part of my heritage. There was a harmony in Rugby League in the North, not only in the team, but with opponents, directors, reporters and especially with the spectators with whom I could now rub shoulders in the club bar and discuss the game and analyse next week's match. After such a good win I could even risk a drink with my father, who had strained for victory on the terraces that afternoon, without fear of too much criticism of my play. I could laugh and joke with old schoolmates who had urged me on. We were all part of such wins.

It is this spirit and comradeship in a northern rugby town, such as St. Helens, that takes great pride in its rugby traditions which can raise it pre-eminent above all others in Britain at certain times of the year. This view may seem romantic to some but it is a true one nevertheless. I have met very few Rugby League players in my career who merely 'played for the money' and the image of the professional, while not being the glamorized version seen by myself in the boys' pen, is certainly not the image of the hard-bitten, insensitive pug many would have us believe. Nevertheless the hopes of such young boys in the pen, coupled with the atmosphere surrounding them in their locality and the support given by their parents, paves the way for their future success as players. These factors have turned St. Helens, Wigan and Widnes into household words and they are also relevant in the achievements of Llanelli, Aberavon and Newport in Welsh Rugby Union. The close-knit community is a vital factor for success. It is the ingredient lacking in the majority of English Rugby Union clubs outside Lancashire, Yorkshire, Gloucester, Devon and Cornwall, where players move from club to club more often and therefore do not have this real sense of belonging and partisanship.

Playing Rugby Union after leaving school in 1958, I had a meteoric and somewhat surprising rise to fame, for within two years I had been selected for Lancashire, England and the Barbarians. But when I converted to League in 1961, so far as St. Helens was concerned, my short career in Union had done nothing to make me a name in the town. The fact that I had been an international at twenty had little significance for them. I was just another apprentice about to be tested as a craftsman, another untried youngster about to have a chance to prove his manhood.

Interchange between the two codes is accepted as a natural part of life in the North. In south-west Lancashire, boys may have played League at the junior school up to the age of eleven and then have gone to a secondary school to play Union to the age of sixteen or eighteen. A boy will play Union for his school on a Saturday and then League for his youth club on a Sunday. While the local Union player will frequently turn out for his works League side on a mid-week evening, the League star can enjoy his social life at the Union club as a social member. I, as an ex-League player, can coach Union at Cowley School, St. Helens, while Steve Tickle, a former Waterloo captain, a product of one of my teams at Cowley incidentally, used to coach League at another school only a mile away. In this atmosphere there is no stigma for the convert from Union to League. Rather it is seen as a natural progression to the top, like moving from non-league to First Division soccer. I welcomed the £5,000 signing-on fee. But the driving force in my decision was the burning desire to meet the challenge and prove my ability to my home town. I also wished to satisfy those ambitions first nurtured as a youngster, cheering home a proud and famous team—St. Helens R.L.F.C.

'Saints officials clinch big deal at midnight' ran the headlines the day after I signed professional in August 1961. That first week of my new career was a rude awakening after the idyllic existence of friendly games at St. Helens Rugby Union Club or Leeds University where one could canter through a match quite comfortably. And it was to be far removed from the 'champers and pâté' of the 'Twickers' car park. No longer would I be addressed as 'French' by the gin-and-tonic brigade at the 'after dinners' at the Mayfair Hotel. I would miss the quaint world of Rugby Union, but I was certainly glad to be relieved of the mental arithmetic needed whenever I claimed expenses for travel. I well remember one famous British Lion who could, by a series of intricate calculations, including tips and claret at Fred's café on the way down, manage to claim £15 for a round trip of a hundred miles hitching! Though I realized that I would have to come to a decision at some time in the future, I pretended not to notice the many League scouts who followed me round the grounds in the 1960/61 season. I was too secure and comfortable at the top of the Rugby Union world and could not steel myself to face the challenge presented by converting to League. I worried and confess to losing many hours of sleep as I wondered what I should do. I was frequently met by my friends in St. Helens with the greeting, 'When are you signing, Ray?' or was constantly quizzed by my student colleagues at Leeds University where I studied for my English degree and teaching certificate from 1958 to 1962. Newspapers devoted columns to the possibilities of certain clubs gaining my signature and whenever I opened my paper in the mornings I seemed to be heading for a new club at greater cost than the day before. Words of advice flowed from Union dignitaries who recommended that I should remain in the Union game and consider my long-term interests.

However, after the last international of 1961 against Scotland, I was approached by Gus Risman, then the coach at Oldham R.L.F.C., in the lounge at the Mayfair Hotel where I was relaxing after the dinner which had followed the Calcutta Cup match. Amid conversation about that afternoon's match I politely turned down his offer but in doing so I knew that I could defer a decision for only a little longer. I had to make up my mind before the forthcoming season, for I could no longer play in such an indecisive frame of mind. I had realized an ambition which had lain dormant in my subconscious since my days as a youngster. Harry Cook, the chairman, and Basil Lowe, the secretary, were extremely forthright and honest and, although never quibbling over the fee, I still had to be convinced by a great friend, Alwyn Williams—ironically a Welshman and the Leeds University full-back—before making my eventual decision.

'Will I make the grade?' This was the question that revolved round my head for hours—'Will I be good enough to play alongside Alec Murphy, Vince Karalius and Tom Van Vollenhoven, the legendary wing? Oh hell, think of it!' I often reflect on how easy it is for a Welshman or foreign player to take his fee, try the game and, if things go wrong, return home without a care in the world. I lived in St. Helens and would also work there. Consequently the pressures on me to succeed were enormous. How could I face the prospect of being a failed Rugby League player in front of old school friends who had accompanied me on my school trips to the Saints' ground as a boy, to Knowsley Road, the mecca of the Northern Union?

'*Daily Mail*, *Herald* and *Express* please.' I bought all the papers eagerly on that August Monday morning but was soon gripped with a fear of the publicity naturally accorded to me in the press. Could I live up to the expectations of my play? I doubted whether anyone could! These thoughts, however, were soon pushed to the back of my mind as I arrived at the club in the evening to be kitted out by the skip man, Walter. He seemed a very blunt and forthright old man, but over the following years he revealed a great pride in the club and a care for every player provided he did not swear in the dressing-room. Walter ruled with a rod of iron over two dingy dressing-rooms, a kit-room and a bath which would welcome attention from the curator of the Roman section of the British Museum—it is the only bath in my experience which requires a five-foot ladder to climb down into it. Yet I would never urge its removal for, like the players who frequented it, the bath abounds in character. How I shrank at the innocent comment of the club chairman as he introduced me over a game of snooker in the clubroom to Dick Huddart, Cliff Watson and Mick Sullivan, all internationals: 'This is Ray French, our latest signing. He's going to be a great player.' Why did he use such words about me in front of these accomplished players who looked me over as a housewife would select a joint of meat from the Co-op? As a product of Cowley School like myself, he was no doubt proud of his protégé but the three players looked at me with a pretended enthusiasm and asked the accepted polite questions usually reserved for royalty on factory visits, all seeking but none daring to ask the size of the fee.

By the time I had watched Sully make a break of twenty-eight, the dressing-rooms below were filling with faces of all shapes and sizes; cut eyebrows, flattened noses and cauliflower ears jostled for space and pegs on the red and cream walls while all eyes were soon centred on R. French vainly trying to melt into a corner in a shroud of self-inflicted modesty and straining to avoid taking anyone's regular peg. Young hopefuls in the 'A' team, signed-on for £10 and obviously suspicious of my value, gazed intently; internationals welcomed me, seeing no threat to their own places, while local-born players such as Bob Dagnall, Wilf Smith and Brian McGinn befriended me most warmly and encouraged me to 'tag along' with them at training. A Rugby League dressing-room has always a warm and friendly atmosphere, breeding deep companionship amid a rich, earthy vein of humour, but there was a chill that night as players were respectful yet cool towards me. Most people like to surround success; few wish to be attached to a failure. I had yet to prove myself.

'You'll take some time to adjust to our standards of fitness in League,' the secretary had said on the completion of my signing, and I was certainly apprehensive of this first training-session. Fortunately the strain envisaged was not to be and I certainly feel that League players, particularly today, are no fitter than top-level Union players, although the game hardens them to a degree never experienced in Union. Our training consisted of fifty-yard sprints punctuated by intense discussions on the photo-finish in the three-thirty race at Kempton Park that day, a few last laps, more discussion on the blonde with the big breasts who had served the drinks in the pub on the way home from Workington, followed by a game of 'tick' rugby. Far from being sceptical of the training, it did not take me long to realize that except for pre-cup runs and pre-season training the intensity and demands of the game were such that this was all that was needed to keep a player in trim and to avoid over-straining in mid-week.

One fascinating aspect of the training evenings was the crowds who used to flock to watch the sessions and who took a close interest in the gladiators performing exercises as if exclusively for their benefit.

'He's not as fast as Dick Huddart.'

'Looks strong though, got a good pair of thighs on him.'

'What about his footballing ability, though?'

These were all typical comments from the touch-line. We paraded as livestock in the ring for their trained eyes, and, being conscious of their close interest, we trained all the harder for their scrutiny. Within two minutes of my stepping off the training pitch that night, the news that I was six yards down on Dick Huddart but was eight yards up on Abe Terry had been flashed by a series of runners, mainly pensioners in uniform of overcoat and muffler, to every town-centre pub. The public would soon be given its pound of flesh, at the current price in my case of £25 per pound. I would be judged against one of the top clubs in the country—Wakefield Trinity—a team in form and capable of assembling a galaxy of stars including Harold Poynton, Alan Skene, the South African centre, Rocky Turner and, as fate had decreed for me, Don Vines. Don had been a great favourite at Saints for a few seasons and I, having been signed to replace him, was now in direct opposition to him in my first senior game.

The scene was set for a 20,000 gate and such a crowd was in evidence as I made my way to the ground in a friend's car. Knowsley Road was full and I was the talking point as the red and white hordes made their way along the roads. The car trip was one of the most nervous of my life as all four

8

occupants sat tight-lipped staring at the crowds lining the pavements. Each one of us was absorbed in his own thoughts. I was conscious of them willing me to succeed, yet realized there was little they could do now except relieve the tension with the odd forced joke. We swung into the players' car park and, having threaded my way through lines of well-wishers and young autograph hunters, I entered the players' door with a Jekyll and Hyde complex, half pleased with myself and half afraid for myself. One of the great blessings of professional rugby was in not having to look after one's kit; I could cast jersey, stockings, shorts and boots to the floor after a game and forget them. Now an hour before the kick-off the clean red and white shirts hung in rows from the pegs; boots, highly polished, lay beneath the bench awaiting their owners. Resin, vaseline, and sal volatile to settle the stomach, all vied with each other for a dominant smell as Tom van Vollenhoven raised himself from the trainer's table, having finished reading the pre-match report in the *Liverpool Echo*. 'What composure,' I thought, 'how could anyone read the *Echo* before kick-off?' How I admired him. It was soon my turn for the 'rub' before the match. The task was then performed by the reserves who slapped, chopped, and rubbed my legs with the guile of a karate novice. Although no masseurs, they helped to prepare the players mentally with their quips and good humour for their skills only served to justify Bob Dagnall's comment: 'Good 'uns don't need it and bad 'uns aren't worth it.' Laughter relieved the tension as old Walter produced a jock strap of rare vintage, obviously worn at the time of the break with Rugby Union in 1896.

'Will this fit, Ray?'

'Do you think he's Errol Flynn?' roared Cliff Watson. 'He could have his bloody tea in it!'

It was passed to me with loving care as though Walter had saved the club from bankruptcy.

'There's more to rugby than playing, you know,' he chortled.

I was urged to wear shoulder pads by Abe Terry, a gentle-voiced coalminer of some sixteen stones who, as an experienced international, seemed to know what he was talking about even though I was arrogant enough to think that I was capable of tackling without them. Six-thirty kick-off was now near as fingers gouged vaseline from the jar and applied it over eyes, ears, and along the chin; gulps of sal volatile were taken from the cracked cup on the window ledge in an effort to calm nerves. Palms were rubbed in the resin on the trainer's bench with all hoping that the awkward low passes would stick. The players were ready; Alan Prescott, the coach, had his say, or at least as much as he could say over the constant chatter of Alec Murphy who always brimmed with confidence on these occasions. The director in charge had given the good news: 'You're on £22 for a win, £6 for a lose.' My first teaching wage had been £17 per week; here I was being offered £22 for eighty minutes' work. Handshakes and good luck were offered to me by all. A friendly nod from Walter and we awaited the 'Big Bang' on the outer door from 'Iron Hand', the gateman who signalled our entry down the dark tunnel into the light and roar of an expectant crowd.

'Take him, Ray, inside, Ray,' screamed Murphy as he marshalled the pack from the scrum-half position. 'Him' was in the shape of Don Vines, now bearing down on me at a great pace, having been put into a gap by Rocky Turner, the Wakefield loose-forward. Here was the classic western confrontation—old campaigner, proud and sensitive of his reputation, and the upstart, proud and eager to make a reputation, 'Thanks, Abe,' I thought to myself as the shoulder pads thudded into his stomach and he fell to the ground. A huge roar came from the crowd for what had been a very ordinary tackle, but it was a roar of relief and encouragement. There was relief for me that they were not super-human players but ordinary mortals with two legs, and encouragement for the crowd who sought early signs of my value. I was now in the game and eager to learn, but what a game it was—a fast, torrid affair with two sent off: Austin Rhodes, the Saints' full-back, and Harold Poynton for tripping Ray French. With the full-time whistle, the score 10-5 in our favour, I was content to have watched the handling skills of the backs, the tackling and the strong runs of the forwards. There was much to learn, but I was in excellent company. 'Good game, Ray, well done, lad, you'll come', were the comments as both teams relaxed in the bath afterwards. Despite the pace and the ferocity, the fouls and the antics displayed on the field, it is amazing how twelve inches of murky water can bind twenty-six players together in mutual respect for each other. Rocky Turner, Wakefield's loose-forward, passed the soap as I washed the blood away from a cut above my eye, the very cut which he had inflicted in a bone-crunching tackle earlier. This was the special flavour of Rugby League which I was to enjoy so much. I felt instantly at home among these tough, friendly sportsmen.

2
Union Trained

Even as a youngster my life was slanted to rugby. Every day
revolved around it. Maths books, with their hard backings,
were the best to use as substitutes for rugby balls in our
never-ending marathon of games played before, during and
after school at Cowley. We would arrive early for an eight
o'clock kick-off with the book suitably rolled up and bound
with a shoe-lace, ready for the start of a game that was to
last through morning break, the lunch hour and on till six
o'clock that evening. During the day our numbers swelled
from three a side to twenty or thirty a side. Here a boy
gained respect not for his seventy-percent mark in history
or physics but for his ability to sidestep off both feet or sell
a dummy to his opponent with only the toilet wall outside
him on the wing. Here the tiny eleven-year-old could play on
the same side as the eighteen-year-old; we could worship our
heroes and develop our talents under their critical eye. We
were forced to play well or we were relegated in shame to a
further 'tick' rugby game on the asphalt surface, reserved for
also-rans and players who did not aspire to the dizzy heights
of playing alongside the school captain. I graduated to these
games when I was ten years old, having played from the age
of seven only on cobblestones and roads for one of our
street teams, McFarlane Avenue Rovers.

With me as manager—it was my ball—we played such
celebrated teams as Fairclough Road Rovers and Dodd
Avenue All-Stars. I look back with astonishment at these
games for we played not in the field but in the road, with
our shirt sleeves buttoned down and handkerchiefs tied
round our knees and elbows to avoid cutting them when we
were tackled. Two sets of gas lamps provided ideal goal-posts
and anybody who has been tackled into a lamp-post on a
cobbled street—although I suppose not many players have
had that experience—will appreciate the pitfalls of these

12

games and the types of player they produced. You became either an insensitive forward or a classical wingman who showed no concern at sidestepping a tree, a lamp-post, or swerving round an ice-cream cart. Why was I a forward? My size and my instincts made me a natural for the position.

All these games of course had been played as Rugby League. It was left to Cowley School to initiate me in the then strange laws of Union, hardly any of us having seen a game. Thanks to the application of Maurice Clifton, a rugby coach who certainly inspired in me the will to win, and a fine headmaster, Walter Wright, who had a passion for the game and who fostered an intense pride in us all, I had quite a successful school career. Perhaps the biggest factor was that at seventeen stones at seventeen years of age I was effective in most school packs. In my early years at school, teams in Lancashire were organized on a weight basis with bantams at 7st. 8lb., and colts under 9st. 8lb., a system which led to many anomalies, with myself being a regular feature. 'Lefty' Lees, a jovial and dedicated school coach of our bantam team, would have two sides assembled on the day of a match, ready to select the 'big 'uns' or the 'little 'uns' depending on the size of the opposition. This policy seemed to satisfy everyone until a 92-0 win at Hutton Grammar School near Preston troubled the master-in-charge and, as a result of his critical comment, Lefty weighed all the team in the canteen after tea. Somehow I and the other prop never appeared on the scales, having left tea early for the coach.

Although my size made me extremely effective at schoolboy level, I soon realized that for club rugby I would need more than a physical frame. Stamina, fitness and pace were necessary if I was to win any honours in the game. This first became apparent in the Easter of 1958 when, while still at school, I was selected to play for St. Helens R.U.F.C. against the local rivals from Orrell, in the last match of the season. Orrell were at that time a junior club, far from being the force they are now, and so were regarded as the right opposition to test a promising schoolboy. It certainly proved a test for I felt all eyes were on me as I staggered from scrum to scrum, and line-out to line-out gasping for air. I had played in the purest of rugby for seven years—schoolboy rugby—and my first experience of the senior game brought about a quick deflation of my ego. From the first illegal push at the line-out to the last dig in the ribs at the final maul, I was battered and bruised by a merciless Orrell pack, who quickly made me realize that the basic difference between club and schoolboy rugby was the physical element. I had been used to towering above my opponents, but was now hacked down with ease and seemed to make little headway against tighter defences. I can well remember a feeling of absolute despair as I trudged from the field with panic-stricken thoughts rushing through my head: 'I'll never make it, it's too hard, it's too fast.'

Despite all the platitudes heaped on me afterwards in the clubhouse, I felt that there was no way I could progress. That I did was a tribute to the St. Helens club and their experienced pack of forwards, who gave me so much help in my early games. However, it was good to be confronted with difficulties immediately on leaving school, for too easy a time can create in a player many faults and weaknesses which may never be removed. A back's pace and skills may shield him from the physical factors of the club game, but the schoolboy forward must adjust to the hardness and tightness of the play very quickly. He either sinks or swims within his first two years.

Though we lacked the incentives of merit-table matches and the John Player Cup, which abound in the game today, there was still a strong element of competition on the field. St. Helens played against the premier sides of the North and frequently contributed players to the Lancashire county team. Most of the players seemed to have an inferiority complex when in the company of more 'socially acceptable' clubs such as Liverpool, Fylde, Wilmslow and Harrogate, but this attitude made us strive even harder to win. This desire to topple the big names brought a sharper edge to our play. Despite this strong sense of competition, the attitude off the field in the fifties was very relaxed and every Saturday was approached with a sense of adventure. Few players knew what time they would arrive home in the evening or even if they would arrive home at all. Club rugby was a way of life. Many of our players presented an amusing picture when arriving for the coach at the Lingholme

Hotel in Boundary Road clad in boiler suits. They had dashed straight from work at Pilkington Glass and all trailed coat-hangers over their backs draped with suit, shirt and tie for the 'night out'.

'Coach leaves at midnight, whether you are there or not,' insisted the skipper who knew very well that he would be leaning against the very same coach door at twelve o'clock in order to count in the married ones returning from supper at the Chinese restaurant or the single ones from the Mecca dance-hall. He might even be placating a local police inspector who was insisting that we pick up three of our members from the station and return the pub sign neatly stowed under the back seat as a souvenir for the club lounge. This easy-going attitude to matches nevertheless produced some outstanding talent who, despite dancing until three o'clock in the morning at the club's New Year's Eve party, could 'turn it on' twelve hours later at Fylde. Nearly all of our players were locals, and most had been to the same school. There was a tremendous enthusiasm for the game in which the skills of our Lancashire backs such as Jim Eccleston, Ken Large, Derek Williams and Tony Leadbetter led Fylde a merry dance. For Fylde it was perhaps just another fixture to be fitted in on a difficult day; for us it was a game to be won, another match which would ease our complexes. Fylde's pitch enabled our club's back play to thrive. Players enjoyed running with the ball, passing and working intricate movements across the field. In the heart of Rugby League country our forwards were expected to handle and run as well as the backs. It was upon this aspect of the game that we concentrated and this provided a solid platform for one feature of my forward play which was to stand me in good stead later as a League player.

It was at Leeds University, however, that I learned the techniques and consciousness of tight forward play so necessary for international Rugby Union. There I became a member of one of the strongest packs of forwards in the North from 1958 to 1960. The university forwards were able to sweep aside much strong opposition and I was able to develop as a second-row.

I was fortunate to play my rugby at Leeds before the end

of the great days of varsity rugby. Rugby clubs at most universities can no longer attract the top-class player, for the growth and attendant publicity of the prestige competitions at club level lure away the exciting prospects who now yearn for something more than a second-class fixture list. University for most people has now become merely an extension to school, with the majority of students being within the eighteen to twenty-one years age-range. Most university sides now lack the steadying influence of the mature students who came from South Africa, Australia and other Commonwealth countries, or those who started at university after two years National Service.

Such players abounded at Leeds in my time and none more so than our wily and experienced captain, Dick Whittaker, who, at the ripe old age of twenty-seven, kept us all in order. Despite having backs of the quality of Fred Hawkins (Wasps and London Counties) and Harry Tolly (the Yorkshire centre), our reputation was founded on the strength of a pack in which three of us were to become English internationals. Two of these were in our formidable front-row of Dave Wrench (Harlequins and England), Ira Hampton (Yorkshire) and Bev Dovey (Roundhay and England). This was one of the strongest front-rows I ever played behind in Union, for all three were as tough as teak, with Dave Wrench being especially ferocious in close-quarter play. Bev Dovey provided inspirational leadership while Ira, at thirteen stones, was a hooker second to none in aggression. They were far from being 'young students at play', and when you place George Waddington Feather at seventeen stones alongside myself at sixteen stones in the second-row, with Dave Jennings, the Yorkshire and Headingley player, at No. 8, we had a pack to be reckoned with. We learned from each other and worked on each other's weaknesses to such an extent that we were able to sweep through our club fixtures with ease and approach the Universities Athletic Union's Cup matches with confidence, though not without some stirring struggles. University rugby was packed with quality players and in the North alone we had Derek Morgan (England No. 8) and Derek Stoneman (England second-row) at Durham University who always provided us with a grand battle, while at Manchester University, the wiles of Bev Risman (England) and Ken Nelson (North-West Counties) presented us with many problems. Such games against Manchester and Durham Universities were fought with keen rivalry. The quality of play was high, too, especially when Leeds played Durham in one U.A.U. qualifying match, for all sixteen forwards were county players. These inter-varsity matches on a Wednesday afternoon were approached with deadly seriousness. Our honour was at stake, and in our Cup rounds of 1960 which led to our appearing against Aberystwyth University in the U.A.U. Final at Moseley's ground we were frequently accompanied by extra bus loads of student spectators all engaged in heated arguments about the team's merits. Despite the Welsh players' attitude that God created them to show the English how to play rugby, we emerged as convincing winners.

Rugby for me has never just been for relaxation. I wanted to win; a casual approach never pushes the player up the ladder to success. But though I was always serious about my rugby, there was plenty of fun in the social round off the field. I well remember the look on a café owner's face when, one night, returning to Leeds after a game in Lancashire, George Waddington Feather dressed in trilby and white mackintosh, and posing as a city detective, shut the poor man's café down for the night over some mythical noise regulations. And the sight of one of my friends sitting in a French railway-carriage en route to Royan and St. Nazaire, and taking an Alka-Seltzer in a bottle of brown ale was an omen for the short tour. This was not the only surprise ingredient on the trip for, having been asked if we would be agreeable to playing a few substitutes in our match with Royan (many years before the subs rule was adopted by the R.F.U.), one can imagine our surprise when at half-time the whole opposition left the field and assembled in front of the main stand. At once fifteen new players in different coloured shirts appeared from the tunnel and lined up for the kick-off. After an enquiry from our secretary, Reg Allington, we learned that the Royan club had thirty players to choose from and since they did not wish to disappoint anyone had decided to play them all. How could we disappoint them? Yet we still won 18-15.

Such escapades provided pleasant relief, but as a player, eagerly seeking the higher reaches of Union, it was vital that I accompany the English Universities' teams on their tours to South Wales. Here, playing against clubs of the calibre of Swansea, Llanelli, and Ebbw Vale, I was beginning to gain the experience needed. I was able to pit myself against the accepted top names of Welsh rugby and was soon to find that they too were only human and that I was able to match them on equal terms. The greatest confidence boost I ever received was while playing for English Universities against Swansea on Boxing Day 1960, just as I was beginning to emerge as a name in English rugby. Despite the many withdrawals from our team which caused us to field a very weak pack, I gained tremendous satisfaction from being able to match the likes of Billy Williams, Norman Gale, John Faull and John Leleu, all Welsh internationals in the Swansea pack, who were intent on giving the 'young English gentleman' his come-uppance. From the first scrum, where a mysterious uppercut appeared to separate our front-row and come looking for me in the second-row, I was a marked man; but how I relished the forward play! This was the rugby I needed if I was not to languish in local club rugby or inter-varsity competition. By the time I was twenty I had been tried and not found wanting. The future it seemed was beckoning me to the top-level competition on which I had set my heart with youthful confidence.

3
Cast Into Stardom

My eyes were firmly fixed on the peaks of Rugby Union, but there was a false crest or two to surmount on the way. For a time ambition outran performance. Indeed, my potential in those early years was well summed up by Alan Clemison of the *Manchester Evening News* who wrote that I was then 'a sound but not inspiring player of seventeen stones who lacked a good deal of stamina'.

Something drastic had to be done if I was to develop as I hoped. I had to lose two stones of flabby weight and in achieving that I like to think I was aided not only by my determination but also by my initiative. Even in the dim light of the St. Helens Rugby Union Club's wooden pavilion few failed to spot a large brown parcel under my arm as I arrived for training one August evening in 1960. In the previous month I had sent for a large rubber suit through a mail-order firm whose advertisement I had read in the paper. With the suit beneath my jersey and a track suit I looked like the Michelin man. Despite catcalls and ribald comment, I trundled on to the pitch to plod the first of many miles throughout the next two months. Although many players nowadays wrap polythene round their waists or wear lighter sweat suits in an attempt to shed excess poundage, I believe the suit which I had was one of the first; and it certainly proved effective, for weight dripped from me at an alarming rate.

In the university vacation I began a policy of training every morning at a local athletics ground, Ruskin Park, and in the evenings at the club, pounding away alone for lap after lap of the pitch. In the morning sessions I concentrated on sprinting and I would frequently be joined by players from the League club doing a stint of extra training. At night I invariably trained alone at the club, for I am afraid the dedication to fitness in Union in the early sixties was not as it is today.

19

Conditions were somewhat primitive at the club in Moss Lane for the sole light was a 500-kw bulb perched high on a flagpole at the end of the pavilion roof giving light only for about forty or fifty yards. Consequently most of the players spent many hours indulging in games of 'tick' rugby. Not that it did St. Helens any harm, as they were among the premier sides in the North in those days with Lancashire players such as Wally Moss, Jim Eccleston and Grahame Twist. Only a few, however, were prepared to hurt themselves running in the dark.

Divine intervention to improve my own play came now in the shape of a serious accident. As a student I was working in a processed foods company in Kirkby, near Liverpool, loading peas into a huge mechanical monster from which they emerged shelled ready for the packet. In the early hours one morning, I was working alongside a spiked conveyor belt. It was cold and I was wearing an old duffel coat which suddenly became caught on one of the spikes of the belt. I was jerked on to the moving conveyor and lay helpless as I neared the vast machinery which would have mangled me to pulp had not a fellow student suddenly realized my predicament and pulled the master switch just in time, saving me from a pea-packet grave. The spikes—in spite of Peter West's assertion much later in the season that I had experienced a 'nasty stomach injury'—had ripped right through my private parts. There was considerable panic as I was duly dispatched to Walton Hospital, while I relaxed in the ambulance turning over in my mind any players whom I could include in my Eunuch's XV for a Saudi Arabian tour. I was reassured by a tall Canadian doctor who, on taking a quick look at me on the way to the operating theatre, addressed me in words as sweet as any offered to Juliet by her Romeo: 'Don't worry, Mac. I'll have a new pair of balls on there in no time.' Twenty-seven stitches later I was restored to normality, but, thankfully, the accident seemed to have a similar effect upon me as I understand it can have on racehorses—I increased in speed by about five to ten yards and won many bets when training was resumed! Within three months, by determination and good fortune I had achieved my target. From entertaining three men and a dog at the local club in early October, I was playing before 50,000 Welshmen at the Cardiff Arms Park in late January, having represented Lancashire and the Barbarians on the way.

If we are to believe the majority of Rugby Union reporters in the national daily newspapers, the average international is expected to spend five or six years gaining experience and maturity before becoming eligible for the national team. Many writers dismiss large numbers of our players with comments such as, 'too young for England yet', or 'not quite experienced enough', whereas Welshmen aged eighteen or nineteen burst on to the scene with the regularity of a Lewis Jones or a Keith Jarrett. Most players who frequent trials or are eternal squad session-men rarely reach the top; I feel that maturity can come suddenly for many players. Certain key games will occur within a short period in which the player will either take his opportunity or lose it for ever. Talent is developed by the company surrounding the player and he can be shot to prominence when thrust at an early age into a quality team. Such a match for me was North-West Counties v South Africa on Wednesday 23 November 1960. A 16,000 crowd had assembled at Maine Road, the home of Manchester City Football Club, to see the Springboks, who had rightly been accorded growing praise as they had stormed their way from victory to victory throughout the British Isles. Their pack, with household names such as props S.P. Khun and P. Du Toit, locks J. Claasson and skipper Avril Malan, and the renowned No. 8, Doug Hopwood, had mastered everything in front of it and they looked a highly fit and organized team. How then did the North-West Counties match up to them? We lost 11-0.

It was obvious to me why they were the best. Although displaying great individual talents, we were totally inexperienced in operating as a unit. To play against the might of South Africa our selected team met only two hours before the kick-off, when we were all introduced to each other. I had never met Mike Evans, the Cheshire second-row. With one hour to go before kick-off we decided who would scrummage on the left-hand side of the scrum and who would pack on the right and who would jump at three or five in the line-out. Our front-row had never scrummaged

21

as a front-row before this game and one was even a regular second-row! Not surprisingly the result of our efforts was seven heels against the head in the first fifteen minutes. Tricky footballers such as Bev Risman, Malcolm Phillips and Bill Patterson, all internationals, never saw a ball as we spent the whole eighty minutes chasing it. Despite all our inadequacies the score was a close one with South Africa having little to offer other than high kicks from Nimb at stand-off and some straight running in the centre from Gainsford and Kirkpatrick—dull, unimaginative rugby which provided Alan Ashcroft and myself with the opportunity to tackle, tackle, and tackle again our way into the England trials of that season. Although I was naturally pleased with our performance at the time, in retrospect we were totally unprepared. As a result of such matches many overseas players established glowing reputations on a very weak platform of opposition from the English sides. I can well understand the South Africans and New Zealanders being upset by our harder approach and better organization in the British Lions' of the seventies, though unfortunately in the 1977 Lions' tour we seem to have taken imitation too far. We have adopted their approach and attitude to the game, but sadly at the cost of sacrificing the traditional flair of British backs.

Today's more thorough approach is reflected in the countless squad training-sessions and coaching weekends following trials matches. In my own trials days we met on the Friday evening before the match and all were expected to live amicably with tomorrow's adversaries. Dining with my rival for the England second-row position was hardly compatible with the competitive attitude I had been brought up on in the North. Exchanging pleasantries with selectors over glasses of orange was hardly conducive to preparing mentally for the trial next day. On such evenings I owed much to another Old Cowleian British Lion, Alan Ashcroft, whose sense of humour and down-to-earth approach certainly settled me. It was he more than any other player who gave me every encouragement both on and off the field, though his own long and celebrated career was coming to its close. He rarely failed to give the correct advice, however blunt.

With David Marques, a specialist line-out jumper, continually beating me at the front of the line-outs in the final trial at Twickenham in December 1960, I could not see myself being selected for the national side. Disconsolate, I turned to Alan, the captain, standing at the back of the line-out in his accustomed No. 8 position. 'What can I do?' I pleaded.

Alan, ever quick-thinking and displaying his shrewd tactical brain, roared back: 'Bloody hit him!'

It proved extremely effective for the remainder of the trial and must have stood me in good stead for, though David Marques was rightly selected, I was named as reserve for the match against Wales in Cardiff.

Before I approached this hurdle, however, I still had a hectic Christmas programme to get through. There were games against Glynneath, Blaina and Swansea for the English Universities before coming into full public view for the Barbarians at Leicester on the Tuesday after Christmas. It was generally accepted that I had been awarded the honour of representing the Barbarians as a consolation for narrowly missing an England cap, but the match was to give the England selectors a further chance to assess my capabilities. Few can have approached such a Barbarians' match in a more hectic manner, for I had played three games in four days prior to the fixture and had left the English Universities' hotel in Swansea at six o'clock on the Tuesday morning to arrive at Leicester in time for the pre-match lunch. As a comparatively unknown youngster, I sat at the table in the company of a team full of internationals, seasoned campaigners of the calibre of Dickie Jeeps, Bev Risman and Ronnie Dawson. Afraid to speak and being extra careful to use the right knife, I managed to stumble through a conversation with Grahame Waddell, the Scottish stand-off. However, such is the spirit and humour in this great touring side that by the time the famous jerseys were handed from an old brown suitcase in the changing-room I felt a seasoned player.

It was in this match that I felt for the first time that the opposition and the spectators were of the opinion: 'Who the hell is this French? What right has he to be playing for the Barbarians?' Deep down inside me there has always been a desire to prove myself to be better than the next man no matter what I am doing, an inner arrogance which I believe is necessary in all players. Nobody south of St. Helens was going to show me how to play rugby. Nor did they. With Vic Harding of Cambridge University alongside me in the second-row I met the Leicester pack head on and, in our 14-5 win, I felt that I more than proved myself on that cold, sunny afternoon. I revelled in the open style of the Barbarians' play and was glad to feed on the short passes of Dickie Jeeps from the tap penalties or follow the breaks of Derek Morgan (England) and Gerry Culliton (Ireland). This match confirmed for me my impressions of two famous players, Ken Scotland and Tony O'Reilly, in that the former was fifteen years ahead of his time as an attacking full-back while the latter's reputation for being an exceptionally strong and powerful runner was fully justified.

And so it was on to the international in Wales, but not before I had played for Leeds University against Nottingham University on the Wednesday prior to the match. I can imagine the cries of horror from today's players who take a week's rest before an international. Moreover, John Currie was now suddenly laid low by flu on the Friday. I was hurriedly drafted into the side as a replacement much to the consternation of writer Terry O'Connor, who followed traditional lines in his cry: 'England gamble with young unknown.' Flurries of telegrams were rushed to our hotel at Porthcawl and many more were awaiting me at the ground on the Saturday morning as St. Helens Rugby Union Club celebrated its new international. The telephone in the hotel foyer never ceased ringing for Mr R. French as rich, earthy, northern voices shrieked down the telephone: 'Give it 'em Ray. Have a good 'un, lad.'

Ray unfortunately was unable to 'give it 'em', for Wales, thanks to two tries from Dewi Bebb, their wing, to a try by our John Young, triumphed 6-3 in a sea of mud. Though the Arms Park at Cardiff was covered in pools of water it did not prevent the Welsh half-backs, Ken Richards and Tony O'Connor, from making many scintillating runs, particularly down the blindside of the scrum. Here they would link up with either Roberts or Davies, the two Cardiff centres, to

24

provide the springboard for Bebb's runs. With Bryn Meredith and his pack heeling the balls from the scrums, we were always chasing the Welsh. But, particularly when the spectators broke into their accustomed singing, I was able, along with Peter Robbins and Laurie Rimmer, to settle into a tackling role. More often than not it was Glyn Davidge, a fine back-row forward, who led the attackers. The singing, however, rather than having an unnerving effect upon me, stiffened my resolve to succeed and proved a great incentive —I would not be beaten, we must not lose. With full-time approaching, Bev Risman made a sidestepping break down the middle of the field and seemed to glide over the mud. He drew Dewi Bebb out of position and in passing to John Young left him with only Terry Davies at full-back to beat. But Haydn Morgan, that red-haired terrier of a wing-forward appeared from nowhere, scythed him down and the danger for the Welsh was over. The crowd roared their approval; the English were out for the count. The whistle sounded loudly as I rose from the last line-out and looked at the delirious crowd on the terraces and heard the ecstatic cries from 50,000 assorted Welsh throats.

'Well done, good win,' was forced from my lips as I shook hands with my opposite number, Danny Harris. 'Liar,' I thought to myself. Tears misted my eyes. I refused to exchange my shirt, thinking, 'It's mine. It might be my last.'

The game was over and I experienced a tremendous sense of relief at not having let myself down. I knew now that I was their equal, I need not fear the star names any longer. I had not let down my friends clustered round their televisions back in St. Helens, and so I strolled quietly from the field. The setting of that match will live in my mind for ever. Here for the first time since leaving school was the atmosphere I had been used to as a boy standing on the League terraces in Lancashire and Yorkshire. It brought an instant recall of the scarves, flags and bunting, the silver hip flasks, the miners clutching their sons and the extra payment for transfer to the 'posh' paddock. Amid the cheers, boos, jeers and singing I thought to myself 'this is Rugby League under Union rules'. Here was the background to create and stir players to greater heights with the fervour of the occasion carried to the player.

At Cardiff Arms Park and also at Lansdowne Road, the home of the Irish Rugby Union, there was real patriotism and a desire for the game, with no social barriers. By comparison, Twickenham, although today attracting a much greater cross-section of society and giving greater vocal backing to the sides, had rather a sedate and 'olde worlde' atmosphere for the player. To play for England is, to me, the greatest honour to which anyone can aspire and the R.F.U. certainly spared no expense and effort in looking after its players in pre- and post-match arrangements. I, like many others, certainly felt elevated on these well-organized England weekends and the R.F.U. as a result gained our respect. Yet, as one was suddenly thrust into what seemed an artificial world after down-to-earth Lancashire, it could prove disconcerting, though mostly amusing, to a young newcomer.

My first sight of the luncheon parties in the Twickenham car park gave me a sense of the unreality of the occasion and, had it not been for the colourful Frenchmen racing in and out of the cars to the accompaniment of blaring bugles and crowing cockerels, I could have been on the grouse moors. It has always seemed strange to me that the 'dear young things' should consider it the height of fashion to be seen eating 'pâté butties' from a car boot in the car park. Still, it all added to the special atmosphere which surrounds Twickenham on the day of an England v France game and I for one was eagerly anticipating the clash with one of the best packs around that season.

The French props Domenech and Roques were regarded by all as fearsome competitors while the back-row—Crauste, Moncla, and Celaya—was acknowledged to be the best in Europe. It was certainly one of the best units I have seen and brought a strong disciplining factor to bear on what proved to be a most voluble pack of forwards, particularly when things began to go astray in the second-half. After a try by Vic Harding, one of three second-row partners for me in that international season (the others being David Marques and John Price), John Wilcox tacked on a difficult conversion to give England a 5-0 lead. Almost immediately the fluent play and snappy handling which is characteristic of a French

26

side gave way to bickering and argument, with the players blaming each other. I well remember laughing at the expression on the hooker de Gregorio's face when he was punched by a team-mate for arriving late at the line-out. We had been forewarned of this in the changing-room by the captain, Dickie Jeeps, and this should have been the moment for pressing home the advantage. But here I feel a selection switch cost us the game. Bev Risman had been switched to play at centre with Richard Sharpe, a fine player but one whose style of play did not suit this occasion, moving into the stand-off berth. In the last quarter of the match we camped inside the French twenty-two-metre line with Richard Sharpe placing well-judged kicks into the open spaces, hoping for our three-quarters to run on to the ball. Vannier, at full-back for France, rose to the occasion and covered every ball, returning it a good thirty or forty yards with his trusty boot. We appeared from scrum after scrum, line-out after line-out, only to see the ball going up into the air and being returned with good measure. The situation surely cried out for some incisive runs and close penetration near the base of the scrum, which I feel Bev Risman could have provided. The French pack was at odds with itself and pressure needed to be exerted on its back-row. If it had been, I am sure they would have collapsed, but as in the manner of many teams who have soaked up considerable pressure for a lengthy time, they hit back. They struck, ironically, with similar tactics to those which failed England, in that Michel Crauste, following up a high kick to our line, snatched a try under our posts. Vannier made no mistake with the conversion and the scores were level at 5-5.

Glory was snatched from us and I felt more deflated than by the loss against Wales. We had striven hard, given of our best, only to finish with a draw—never a satisfactory result for a player. The French spectators raced on to the Twickenham pitch at the final whistle. Their honour had been saved while we were left to reflect on what might have been. Even the luxury of the large individual baths in the Twickenham changing-rooms could not wash away the empty feeling of a draw—a sort of no-man's-land in international rugby. Nevertheless, after an hour in which we had bathed, changed and drunk a cold beer, we were speeding on our way by coach, singing merrily, to the after-match dinner at the Mayfair Hotel. On such a journey to the hotel players are slowly beginning to assess their performances and often scan the first editions of the evening newspapers hoping for a good mention. Others seek reassurance from a friend as to the quality of their game, and most wonder and hope that they have played well enough to be selected again. Many hover close by any stray selector who, in an offguard moment, might say the words which would make or mar a player's dinner.

From my first arrival in London for the match against France, I was more than slightly overawed with the people surrounding me. I had, as I thought, already prepared my impeccable background for the match programme and any pre-match publicity. When asked to provide details of myself one of the questions concerned my hobbies. At that time rugby was my only pursuit save cards and darts in the local at home, but thinking that skiing and squash sounded better I inserted these in the pre-match publicity, much to the amusement of my friends. Little did I know the predicament I would be placed in at the cocktail reception prior to the dinner at the Mayfair.

'Ah, I see you're a skier, French.' He was an administrator, I was a player.

'That's right,' I said, blushing to the very roots. 'What the hell is he going to ask me?' I thought.

'And where do you ski?' asked the guest with a polite smile.

This was indeed a tricky question for I had never stood upon a pair of skis in my life and, apart from St. Moritz which I dismissed from my mind as being too obvious, I was unfamiliar with the name of any Alpine ski resorts. Inspiration finally struck.

'On the lower slopes of the "Bergi",' I replied, refraining from adding that the 'Bergi' is the name of the Pilkington Glassworks dump for broken glass in St. Helens.

He nodded his approval and added that he would ask his travel agent about it. Sipping my drink I moved on to speak to the Lord Mayor of London, Sir Bernard Waley Cohen;

in my black shoes loaned by the St. Helens coach driver and looking resplendent in my evening suit, neatly pinned at the waist and borrowed from the coach owner, Stan Mogowan, I had the feeling of being 'born to this life'.

It was indeed a grand life but the real pleasures were gained from playing in the company of some of the best players in the world at that time, especially in an England team which had some young blood in the shape of Bev Risman, Budge Rogers, Derek Morgan and myself nicely balanced with older established men such as Dickie Jeeps, the captain, and Ron Jacobs in the pack. Many were to become established stars themselves but one for whom I had the greatest respect was Derek Morgan, who unfortunately suffered damage to a knee which considerably shortened his career. He was a fine tactician, rough and aggressive on the field with a sound pair of hands, so necessary for the No. 8 position. He would have made an excellent loose-forward in Rugby League. Of the opposition, Dave Hewitt, the Queen's University and Irish centre, was the equal of any centre I have seen playing Union—a natural footballer, a shrewd judge of a gap, and very fast. With his skilled footwork, for me he could have been one of the truly great centres, but he seemed somewhat too shy and too retiring for the demands of the game. To play against men such as Crauste, Celaya, and Moncla, the celebrated French back-row, Bryn Meredith, the tough Welsh hooker, and Sid Millar and Hugh McLeod, the Irish and Scottish props, certainly brought an edge to my play as a forward. With the end of the internationals, however, I was soon faced with the deflation of playing bread-and-butter rugby against local opposition in front of a handful of people for the remainder of the season.

While many clubs and their players benefit greatly from the presence of an international in the side, I felt that in my case I had very little to gain from playing with, by national standards, a junior club. I was extremely happy at St. Helens in the company of my ex-schoolfriends and would never have left the club had I remained in the Union game. But, having tested the excitement of the Arms Park and Twickenham, I was hardly filled with enthusiasm when boarding the coach on blustery cold Saturday mornings in March for the delights of Rochdale or Kendal. There was little at stake in end-of-season rugby in the sixties.

Although I understand the moans of some spectators about competitive rugby, and the problems now confronting the R.F.U. over its implementation, what a blessing it must be for a player to play in merit-table matches, county and national cup matches, with something more at stake than friendlies every Saturday. When Wigan Rugby League Club have to keep an eye on Orrell Rugby Union Club's fixture list for fear of clashing with a cup match, a situation undreamed of ten years ago, the players involved must have a sense of occasion and must be all the fitter and keener for it. I would be overjoyed to play Union with its present outlook, for my only chances to play at a higher level came in the many charity matches or guest XVs which abound in the game. By the end of the 1960/61 season I had notched up seventy-five games, an average of over two matches a week for the season.

The dedication of men such as Stuart Faulds, who runs the Anti-Assassins team—a guest XV playing matches for charity—is to be admired, while teams such as the Public School Wanderers, especially in matches against school sides, perform a valuable service to the game. In the North, the Anti-Assassins are most active, none keener and more knowledgeable than Stuart himself. But even he was taken aback recently when I questioned him on the history of his guest XV. 'Who was the only Rugby League international to score three times in a Rugby Union match against the Anti-Assassins?' That floored him. Little did he know that the incident had had its beginnings back in my days at Leeds University when we had been asked to provide a side to play at Bury against them. At nine o'clock on a Sunday morning, as we waited under the tower of the Parkinson building in Leeds, we were one short—a familiar situation for our university teams.

'Where can I get a player this early on a Sunday morning?' Club secretaries will know the feeling as the awful terror grips them that they might even be forced to turn out themselves! We had only one alternative. Gerry Round, a fellow student of mine and then the Wakefield Trinity and Great Britain Rugby League international, lived close by with another of our team. He was instructed to play under the name of Gerry Higgins and was advised to be careful during the game.

'Take things easy in the centre, Gerry, feed your wing all the time and nobody will ever know.'

After scoring three tries and making two for his wingman, all in the clubhouse looked upon him after the game as 'a fine prospect', and wondered why he had not featured in the Yorkshire trials that season. None was more delighted than the Rugby League scout from the Leigh area who raced across the pitch after the game and, flinging his arm round his shoulders, offered him trials for the following Saturday.

'You can earn a lot of money in our game, son,' he assured him. 'Here's my card. Give me a ring next week.'

My playing career in Union was brief, spanning only three seasons in senior rugby, but my rise to the top level was meteoric. Naturally I was most grateful to the Union game for the lessons it had taught me. Few players are sufficiently gifted, and it made me realize the necessity for hard work both on and off the field. Without total dedication and application off the field the rewards are few on it. The high standards of the game then, now sadly in decline, taught me the benefits of personal discipline as a key attribute for a player. The ability to step back mentally on a field, survey the whole scene unswayed by emotion and then make the necessary tactical adjustments, is a priceless asset. Union, with its greater technical complexity and more static situations, enables one to develop this ability. Although I was about to cross the great dividing line to 't'other side', the next ten years were to see me in the unusual position of straddling both codes as I pursued my own career with St. Helens Rugby League Club and then with Widnes, while at the same time becoming immersed in the world of schoolboy Rugby Union. How I underestimated the influence and impact of schoolboy rugby upon me. It was to become a consuming passion, the most rewarding and gratifying part of my whole career in rugby. But that was the last expectation in my mind as I anxiously weighed the pros and cons of changing codes. The only motivation to break with

Union was pride of performance. With my background, I had to prove to myself and to my home town that I was man enough for League rugby. That was the ultimate challenge which I could no longer shirk.

4
The Lure of League

Money was not the object of my transfer to League, but the subject obsessed some players and spectators. 'How the hell can they turn all that down, Ray? They must be bloody mad.' That was a typical comment from one of our hardened professionals at St. Helens as he pointed to the headline in the evening paper—'Rugby Union star rejects Salford's £15,000 offer.' 'I got £100. Wish I'd played Union,' was often the accompanying remark. To explain to a player steeped in the traditions of the League game since the age of seven, and without any background of Rugby Union, was indeed difficult. To explain the financial principles behind the rejection was even harder. To a prominent Union player, whose future is being mapped out by the club president's offer of a partnership in the firm, or who is about to rise rapidly in the world of public relations at the drop of an international cap, the sum of £5,000 cash, to be followed by £2,000 for every season completed with the League club, does not appear such a glamorous offer as is often imagined. Such generous-seeming offers help to provide glamour and publicity for the game, but they are few and far between, at most two or three a year.

While not discounting the powerful influence of the many great players signed from the Union game, the fact is that the majority of League players will have come from the local schools. So the local Union player has not only the financial gain to influence him in transferring to League, but also the desire to prove himself within the local community. Certainly my main motivation was the need to test myself, the feeling that I could not be judged as a rugby player until I had proved myself at both codes, and particularly the one most respected in my home town. That might sound strange to the southern player or the Welshman who has come up from the valleys for financial security. But

33

I firmly believe this sense of challenge is a main factor in many players' conversion as it was in mine. Certainly in discussions with Peter Harvey (Lancashire R.U. and St. Helens R.L.F.C.), I found his feelings identical to my own when he decided to sign. We were returning to a game which had been at our roots before the age of secondary schooling removed us from it. Few people outside the four counties of Lancashire, Yorkshire, Cumbria, and, since the reorganized boundaries, Cheshire (I still cannot believe in Widnes as part of the 'Cheshire set') realize that here only one or two schools, usually based on the old grammar school or the new sixth-form college, actually play Union. At junior and secondary level some fourteen to twenty schools per town engage regularly in Rugby League, each town having its own cup and league programmes for the season. The traditions of the towns and the sporting interests of the boys' fathers, with the endless discussion of the League game in their clubs and at work, will direct a boy to the professional club. Lord Pilkington has regularly admitted that a bad season for the Saints is reflected in falling production figures on the shop floor at Pilkington Glass. Clubs therefore should have a steady supply of local schoolboy talent and they can keep in close contact with the better players who will be absorbed into their Under-18s or Colts' sides.

I say 'should have' for I fear that over the past twenty years schoolboy Rugby League has been one of the biggest weaknesses in the League game, and I must be highly critical of many of my fellow schoolmasters. While the popularity of town cup competitions has thrived, only thirteen to twenty players in five or six matches per season have been catered for, and all the effort is channelled into a very narrow area. As a result, the number of matches per year-group at many schools has amounted to no more than a dozen per season. If a team is the best in the town at the Under-12 level, they will not be any the more developed by playing the same teams for the next five years. Greater emphasis should have been put on individual schools developing regular fixture cards, as is done in the Union-playing schools, and on attaining regular inter-town or county fixtures and tours abroad. When Cowley School could play 176 games at all age-levels in the season 1975/76 in areas as far apart as London, South Wales, Hereford, Yorkshire and Canada, and the figure for all games played between all the other schools in St. Helens could scarcely match that, then something is wrong. Although they need greater help from the major clubs, schoolmasters should give up their moans of lack of finance. You can always collect some waste paper, sell jumble, organize dances and raffles, or sell Christmas cards to raise the necessary money. I well remember the argument I once had with Bill Johnson, a member of the Lancashire R.L. committee, and a staunch and dedicated worker for the game, when he accused me of undermining the League game even though I was taking payment for playing it. On my first teaching appointment, at Fairfield High School, Widnes, I was confronted with a situation where many boys were over age for schools' rugby (the limit at that time being fifteen) and where the other age groups were playing only four or five matches a season against the other two secondary schools.

Consequently, I did what any self-respecting schoolmaster should do. I organized and coached the boys in both codes by playing League matches in mid-week and Union matches at the weekend, with the result that they were then able to play some twenty to thirty games in each year-group. The drift to the haunts of Liverpool and Manchester soccer clubs was stopped and the interest in that game was halted. That every one of the secondary schools in Widnes has followed suit within the last ten years has surely proved my point. It mattered not which code they were playing but that they were playing with an oval ball and not with the round variety. Successful signings from their own schoolboy ranks have surely not indicated any undermining of Rugby League as in the cases of Bentley, Hughes, Derbyshire, Bowden and O'Neill. The healthy state now of schoolboy rugby in the town, coupled with the phenomenal rise since 1976 of club and pub teams for schoolboys, has given the Widnes club a sound basis. I believe the weaknesses have at last been noticed by the new administration at League headquarters and the introduction of seven-a-side competitions by senior clubs in the half-time interval gives schoolboys the thrill of playing before a large crowd. The curtain-raiser games for Under-11s before the Wembley Cup Final coupled with the welcome rise in the number of junior schools playing the game augurs well for the future. The fact that over 150 schoolmasters have now qualified as graded coaches since the inception of a coaching scheme a few years ago proves we are moving on the right lines again.

Ex-schoolboy stars will possibly play a season or two as an amateur with the Colts' side of a professional club, but many will gain their experience the hard way, playing professionally in the 'A' team where, thanks to a combination of young aspiring debutants and old warhorses who know all the tricks of the trade, a boy's career will either be made or broken. The failure rate for players between the ages of sixteen and twenty is high. For, unlike football with its apprentice system, they are at once treated as equals and many may not develop the physical qualities required or possess the dedication and application needed to succeed. A try scored by a sixteen-year-old still counts the same three points—a try missed can cost a winning pay bonus. No favours can be held out to the youngster. He must learn to take the knocks and give them back.

Nevertheless, every July and August young hopefuls will still arrive for training with the first-team squads, some nervous, some cocky, all hopeful of catching the eye on a Tuesday or Thursday evening. Their fees are measured in terms of hundreds rather than thousands of pounds but all are keen to be the next Alec Murphy or Frank Myler at St. Helens or Widnes. The chances of gaining a place in the first-team is their motivating factor, not money, and pre-season training is often refreshed by their innocent outlook. In my playing days the first- and second-team players at both clubs tended to change in separate changing-rooms, yet all the sprinting, lapping, and exercises were done together. Such youngsters frequently brought a competitive edge to the training, for many relished the opportunity to prove themselves faster over fifty-yard sprints than the first-team wing, or to try to match the weight-lifting capacity of the regular prop. Their presence in the early pre-season training, even if many do fall away rapidly, is good for the

game, because training in the company of established internationals with household names has a tremendous effect
on the lads and fosters their ambitions. No 'old stager'
likes to be upstaged by a fresh-faced youngster just recruited
from the local school and he is thus forced to run all the
harder to maintain his image. A two-hour session at Widnes
could be quite hectic if I was paired with a couple of new
teenage recruits, who, eager to impress, could work up a
heavy sweat for a seasoned campaigner like myself yearning
for an end to the night's physical exertions.

Towards the end of my career in the early seventies, at
Widnes, when training had been completed and most of the
players had soaked in the bath until nine o'clock, I would
often be greeted in the room reserved for players above the
changing-rooms by Tommy Shannon, a great half-back in his
playing days: 'Saved you a couple of ham butties, Ray.
Pickles are on the table. Brian's been at 'em again.' Tommy
was the skipman who, ever smiling, would pour a refreshing
cup of tea from behind the small hatch in the corner near the
stairs and, like many of the ex-Widnes players, continued to
give faithful service to the club. A motley collection of
electricians, sales representatives, teachers, labourers,
scaffolders, clerks and trainee accountants would all be found
here, relaxing after a hard session of training, usually
reflecting on the last game, team selections or the bonus
for the coming week's match. Many had come straight
from work in their oil-stained overalls and would be
changed now into their suits or casual clothes but would
not return home before grabbing a bite to eat. A few
would eat their last meal before drinking a couple of pints
in the local, The Albion, as a prelude to an eight-hour shift
at the factory. I wonder how many of our highly paid and
pampered soccer players would relish an eight-hour shift
after training!

Many a time after an exhausting day's teaching, followed
by a school rugby practice or society meeting, I rushed to
Widnes or St. Helens in the car for a prompt six-thirty start.
Frequently weary, but knowing it had to be done, I enjoyed
training nights not only for the amount of physical work
demanded but for the constant banter and humour of a

dressing-room—often better than a night at the music-hall. Some players are natural trainers, while others are less inclined to exert themselves in mid-week. Tommy Bishop, Jim Measures and Kel Coslett were all examples of players, in my time at St. Helens, who could continually force themselves and who seemed to gain real satisfaction from running. Others, such as John Tembey and Dick Huddart, two Cumbrian internationals, could coast through training yet still look extremely fit and be more effective than some of us who had run until exhaustion. Each man's attitude and temperament was different. Vince Karalius, surely one of the finest of Great Britain's loose-forwards and the yardstick by which forwards must be measured, is reputed to have run from his home in Widnes, a distance of some six miles, before training and to have run the distance home when he had completed his stint. A hard man.

By seven o'clock the Saints' dressing-room would be emptying for a game of touch rugby before actual training started. Only a few malingerers, who did not relish the wind and rain after a hard day's work, remained inside, taking their time to adjust their boots. It is amazing how on some foul nights half an hour could be wasted over sorting my socks or hunting for a new jock strap. The coach, Joe or Stan, would frequently return to the dressing-room frustrated at being unable to drag a clever malingerer from its warmth or to eject a seasoned campaigner, basking under the heat of the lamp on the physiotherapist's bench. Many hours could be spent under the lamp removing a 'twinge' at the back of a leg. Unsuccessful, the coach would make his way out again, stopping to peer through the steam rising from an early bath being taken by the injured, who had only come for a hot bath, a check on the injury with the doctor and to pick up the pay packet from the last match. Injuries rarely last long in League as all clubs adhere to the principle of 'no play, no pay'. And apart from some small industrial compensation payments the player must be playing to gain his wage. I have known collar bones heal quicker than from a trip to Lourdes.

Since League is essentially a handling game, with the kicking of the ball kept to a minimum, the emphasis in training is on work with the ball. We indulged in endless games of touch rugby or, when practising as a team, unopposed rugby. Such simulated games with no opposition provided opportunities for working at set moves from 'play the ball' situations, where a player guides the ball back to one of his own side after a tackle, to tap penalties. It also allowed us to concentrate on the positional play of both forwards and backs. This form of rugby is particularly effective for forwards in League whose role requires running with the ball to a far greater extent than in Union. The ball-skills in handling and distribution expected of the big men can only be gained and developed by split-second timing at close quarters in such games. Its most glaring weaknesss is a lack of opposition and a physical presence. Don Gullick at Widnes in the 1970-72 period is the only coach I have seen encourage tackling in training to good effect, often joining in himself. Under Don, a player could easily be injured as he expected you to train as you played. Defences in the League game lie up very flat on their opponents and many breaks are sparked off by an individual burst or a piece of improvisation. Pace is the essential quality needed by all players and therefore after an initial half-hour's interval running, lapping the field and exercising as a warm up, the bulk of the evening would be spent in sprinting. Both Saints and Widnes were fortunate to have cinder areas outside for sprint work, but St. Helens especially so, for they also possessed a sixty-yard sprint track beneath the main grandstand which was ideal for training in bad winters.

The track was complete with sets of starting blocks and it was here that Stan McCormick, the coach in my 'apprentice' days at the Saints and a former professional sprinter himself in his playing days, concentrated his efforts. He continually stressed the need for speed off the mark. Such sprinting, which was usually done in groups of four, was highly competitive and many arguments raged over a false start as we did not wish to appear down on one of our contenders for a first-team place. Since the custom was for players to run according to position, the competition could really hot up if four second-rows were running together and all four were in competition for a first-team place. It is easy to see why Alec Murphy was able to reign for so long as a supreme half-back, for, despite all his other mercurial skills, even Tom Van Vollenhoven, the flying South African wing who had clocked 9·7 seconds for the 100 yards, could scarcely pull away from Alec over the first twenty yards. The track was invaluable when snow was on the ground and particularly so in the winter freeze-up of 1964 when little rugby was played for nearly two months.

Changing and then relaxing in the hot and steaming bath is one of the great pleasures of life, but it was also the entertainment in the dressing-rooms that made training worth while. On some evenings these would resemble a bazaar, with players 'in the know' selling all manner of goods which had 'fallen off a lorry'. Lengths of cloth for suits, bars of scented soap and large bath towels (as long as you did not mind 'National Coal Board' stamped on them). Occasionally, however, the seller did not get such a bargain, as in the season when Saints signed a man who could supply gents' clothing at reduced prices from out of a large suitcase, which he was accustomed to bring with him to training. He had a ready customer one night when a player said: 'I'll have two pairs of socks, two shirts, a tie and a pullover. Do you mind if I settle up with you on Thursday night when I get paid?'

The amateur salesman rummaged through the suitcase and came up with a very nice matching shirt and tie to suit the brown pullover tucked underneath his arm. 'All good stuff this,' he confirmed. 'Certainly, pay me on Thursday.'

Imagine his dismay when the buyer was transferred to Yorkshire on the Wednesday morning.

When transactions closed, the dressing-room would ring with the talk of transfer fees and who was 'unsettled' and why. The term 'unsettled' can cover a multitude of sins and is usually taken by the public to mean that a player currently out of favour for selection is seeking a transfer. This was often the case and the club chairman had to be available at all times to see his 'unsettled' players. Harry Cook, then the St. Helens club chairman, would listen patiently to the player recently returned from an Australian tour with the Great Britain party who was short of money for the new mortgage and who now required a 'backhander', the professional jargon for an extra payment. A player with

family or personal trouble might require a quick move from
the club to another county. All would plead their case
upstairs in the boardroom where Harry, in a serious face
reserved for such occasions, would say for the three-
hundredth time: 'We can't. Gates are bad and we just haven't
the money at the moment. Anyway, we still can't. It's illegal,
against the League's laws.'

The humour and spirit of the night would be shattered at
St. Helens by the entrance of the coach carrying a single
sheet of paper on which was printed the thirteen names to
play that Saturday. Frequently it was not the team he
desired, for often this was changed by the directors. He
would pin the sheet on the solitary notice board at the side
of the physiotherapy room and make a darting movement
into the little room as if trying to avoid the gaze of his
players. Who would be upset this week? Who had the
directors left out? How could he explain it to the player who
desperately needed to keep up the payments on his new car?
He would have to. Regulars and established players, in the
act of fastening a tie or rubbing themselves down with a
bath towel, announced their confidence in selection by a
nonchalant enquiry to a bystander at the notice board. 'What
time does the coach leave on Saturday?' 'Where are we
stopping for dinner?'

Youngsters, seeking their first game, rushed to the board,
their hearts pounding at the thought of playing, but all
aiming not to show too much excitement if selected. Those
on the fringe, or unsure of their places, sidled up to the board
and casually combed their hair in the small mirror at the side,
with one eye straining to read the team sheet. Some strolled
away disconsolate to gather in huddles for the inevitable
criticism of the selected team, rolling out the well-worn
clichés. 'He won't bloody have it when it gets hard.' 'What
has he done since he came here?' 'Flu? I've never known him
play at Workington yet.'

More voluble players would seek out the coach, vainly
hiding behind the boot-cupboard door, and in raised voices
'discussion' would frequently take place as to their non-
selection, usually followed by a string of obscenities and the
final defiant gesture: 'You can stuff it. I'm seeing the

41

chairman.' More trouble for Harry.

The coach, whether it was Stan, Joe, or Alan, was in an impossible position trying to satisfy thirty to forty players, each with his personal opinion of his own ability. Having to endure the criticisms and carping remarks of those 'twelve apostles', the directors, and with the spectators ever on his back, his was a thankless task. Rarely in full control of selection, rarely in command of the buying and selling practices at the club, he was a lonely ping-pong ball batted between player and director, success and the inevitable failure. Six different coaches in my ten seasons as a League player indicate the rapid turnover in this most thankless of jobs. But these were the men who helped me to establish myself at the anxious start of my League career and who maintained my personal drive to improve.

5
At Home with St. Helens

It was a relief for me when the thinking and the talking ended and I had finally taken the plunge into League rugby. My signing of forms had taken such a time because I had been filled with many doubts about my likely success at the game. But I was in no doubt over choosing St. Helens as my club. It was no secret that I was pursued by others and had turned down an offer higher than St. Helens had promised. In considering a career in the League game I looked forward to many seasons in the sport, and Saints, with their proud record, seemed the best prospect for a future. I could not have chosen better, for St. Helens continued their policy of buying Union players to complement their own local talent, a policy which began in earnest with the Welsh influx of George Parsons, Ray Gale, Glyn Moses, Steve Llewellyn and Don Gullick. We were rarely out of the headlines, for the best clubs attract the best players, and I was indeed fortunate in having teams of many talents round me during my seven seasons there. These were teams which won every cup and honour in the game many times over and certainly brought me financial rewards which more than compensated for the lower fee I accepted when signing for the Saints.

There should be no illusions regarding the financial rewards available to the professional player—few are able to cruise to the Caribbean for their holidays. Although it has often been mooted by distinguished commentators on the game that a fully professional sport with approximately twenty clubs would raise the standards of play, the traditions of League have always been rooted in the part-time professional with each player having a normal occupation. Training on two nights of the week followed by a game at the weekend fits admirably with the electricians, teachers, drivers and bank clerks who make up a typical team, each realizing that he cannot live off the game alone and looking upon

43

League as a means of gaining the extras in life.

In my ten seasons of League from 1961 to 1972 I never had the good fortune to receive more than £1,000 in any one season with a club, though experiencing more success than the majority of players. Since upwards of a third of such payments are taken by taxation, the remaining figure of some £700 for more than forty games a season is hardly a fortune. The rewards today for those in a very successful side will possibly approach £4,000, but the difference between success and failure is staggering. Winning pay and losing pay can often differ by as much as £65 for a victory to £15 for a defeat. The incentive to win in League is paramount. My winning payment at Wembley in the Cup Final against Wigan in 1966 was £100, but had Wigan won this would have shrunk to £15 less tax. It is also imperative to play regularly because a player is only paid if he plays. A serious injury, or even minor ailment, can not only cost a player his place in the team but jeopardize his finances should he also be unable to go to work. The situation can and often does occur whereby a player loses his wages and often his job through injury. I well remember the predicament in which George Nicholls, the Great Britain second-row, was placed when Widnes decided to play their games on a Sunday afternoon. While the changeover suited schoolmasters like myself, to George, handsomely paid for Sunday work as a scaffolder at a power station, it meant a big loss of money. Needless to say the rugby won. I have met very few men who only played the game for the money. Many moan at the injuries, some protest at the bonus, but the majority has an inner passion to play.

With added sponsorship in the form of man-of-the-match awards, or player-of-the-season cheques, the pay is at least far greater than the sums available to the glassworker or miner of St. Helens and Widnes at the turn of the century. Those early dissidents who found it financially impossible to work and play, and who engineered the break with the Union game over the question of 'broken-time payment' (expenses for loss of work on match days) had little idea that they would pave the way for the likes of myself, John Mantle, John Warlow, Kel Coslett and others.

St. Helens R.L.F.C., founded in the 1870s by a German chemist named Herman for the recreation of the workers at Pilkington Glassworks, was first captained by a Frenchman called Le Paton. A few years later, during the 1890s, the club was at the centre of developments which eventually saw rugby split into two codes. Union clubs in the north of England faced difficulties with many of their players over broken time and soon came into conflict with their headquarters who were afraid of professionalism creeping into the game. After earlier attempts by Yorkshire representatives to raise the matter with the Rugby Union, a meeting was held at the George Hotel in Huddersfield on 29 August 1895 with twenty-one clubs present. All, with the exception of Dewsbury, resigned from the Northern Rugby Union. Saints and Widnes were among these forerunners, and St. Helens played their first match under the auspices of the Northern Union against Rochdale on 7 September 1895, a week before the opening of the official Union season. This was a shrewd move on the part of the early administrators of the game, for these early matches attracted average gates of 6,000 people. The broken-time payments were fixed at six shillings but the fears of the Union officials were soon realized when, with over eighty clubs in membership and the game booming, the wealthier and more successful clubs began to give their players much higher payments. St. Helens had the good fortune to play in the forerunner of the modern Challenge Cup Final against Batley on 1 May 1897 before a crowd of 16,000 at Headingley, Leeds. When they lost 10-3 the local St. Helens press was most critical of the long train journey from St. Helens to Leeds being followed by the team's four-mile drive in a horse-drawn cart to the ground. The size of the Saints' pack must surely have also had some effect, average weight and height being 12 st. 4 lb. and 5 ft. 8 ins.

The game was still played according to Union rules with only the line-out being abolished. It soon prospered in the towns of the North to the extent that by the 1888/89 season the first fully professional teams were competing with each other. St. Helens, who suspended a player for two months for failing to work in mid-week, had a special clause inserted to see that all players had a regular job. It was the St. Helens Club again who, in 1902, were at the centre of the movement's most revolutionary step. Following their suggestion, it was agreed to have only thirteen players a side and the teams organized into two divisions. St. Helens were indeed lucky to be admitted to Division One that September. Despite finishing next to the bottom of the table the club seems to have been financially stable. The prospects for the future were more secure when they moved from Littlers Fields to Bishop Road and thence to Knowsley Road, the present home, acquired in 1890 at an annual rent of £30 10s. from a Mr. Samuel Taylor. He insisted, however, that they allowed the local farmers the use of the manure depository at the side of the pitch.

Up to the time of the First World War the club enjoyed only mediocre success, but in Jim Turtill, signed from New Zealand, J. Houghton, one of the first managers of an Australian tour in 1910, and J. May, who refereed three Cup Finals in 1911, 1913, and 1914, the town certainly had personalities who contributed to the growth of the game. The two best-known characters of the day must surely have been the Rev. C. M. Chavasse, who later became the Bishop of Rochester, and Matt Creevey, who was a world-champion long-jumper. Chavasse, a flying wing, was selected to run in the 1908 Olympic Games and is possibly the only bishop to play League, while Matt Creevey is reputed to have cleared vast numbers of beer barrels in his trick repertoire and is on record as having jumped nearly twenty feet to the line when a defender was closing in on him. Characters all, but even they could do little to halt the march of the Huddersfield team of 'all-stars' in the Cup Final of 1915 when Saints were defeated 37-30. This temporary lift from mediocrity was again accompanied by a most interesting press comment to the effect that there would have been a much bigger crowd than the 8,000 attendance if the match had been played at Wigan or any other place within walking distance.

With the virtual shutdown of the game during the First World War, the club soldiered on until the Earl of Derby opened a new pavilion and dressing-rooms before a crowd of 22,000 on 27 December 1920. The team played old rivals Wigan in the new colours of white shirts and black shorts, the Earl's racing colours. There then followed a period of consolidation before the glory years from 1925 to 1932. During this period, the quality of the side was such that seven players, Albert Fildes, Oliver Dolan, Frank Bowen, Leslie Fairclough, Alf Ellaby, Alf Frodsham and Ben Halfpenny, all from the town of St. Helens, toured Australia in 1928. Two of the town's greatest stars were undoubtedly Leslie Fairclough, the complete half-back, who was signed when an army drummer-boy for half-a-crown, and Alf Ellaby, one of the finest wingmen ever to play rugby, who scored over 487 tries in his career. Despite such players and the New Zealand 'H' trio of Hutt, Hall and Hargraves, the club was still unable to win the coveted Challenge Cup being defeated 3-10 by Widnes at Wembley in 1930.

It was after the Second World War that the club's policies were to bear fruit. By entering the transfer market in a big way with the purchase of English, Welsh and South African Rugby Union talent, the directors and coaches were able to add to the extraordinary skills of local players such as Austin Rhodes, Alec Murphy, Duggie Greenall and Jimmy Honey. Consequently, the last twenty-five years in the club's history have been the equal of any team's in Rugby League with the elusive Challenge Cup coming back to the town on no less than five occasions.

The Challenge Cup and the Championship Final are the lure for all players and spectators. In the size of crowds attracted, the play and attitude of the players, something of the special atmosphere is experienced which gives League a flavour all of its own. Lacking the cosmopolitan background of the larger city soccer clubs in Liverpool, Manchester and London, the close proximity of the towns and the traditional inter-Pennine rivalry produce an intense local pride giving rein to a unique competitiveness. I certainly appreciated this atmosphere, its tensions and the satisfactions it brings at those crucial times of a season when rugby became my life to the exclusion of all else.

To be confronted with Hull Kingston Rovers, one of the strongest of Yorkshire sides, in the third round of the Rugby

League Cup on an April evening in 1966 was no easy task, even though we had gained the home advantage. To be losing 7-10 and the game well into extra time was, however, a shock to the 19,000 fans fervently checking and re-checking their watches. Having beaten Wakefield away by 10-0 and Swinton at home by 16-4 in the first two rounds we had been expected to march triumphantly to Wembley. But, perhaps through over-confidence, here we were playing haphazardly and hopes of seeing the twin towers were slipping away fast. 'How have they gone on? Have they won?' were the questions being asked in the surrounding pubs and clubs as hordes of depressed and furious fans streamed into the bars, discarding banners and rosettes as if they were some mark of disfavour. All had left the game a few minutes before the end to avoid the traffic congestion. 'They've done it again. Lost! They allus promise so much then let you down.' 'They're not worth bloody watching, that's me finished for this season.' Even bingo numbers ceased as the score of 7-10 was announced over the caller's precious microphone. But few reckoned on the intervention of Alec Murphy and the biggest slice of luck—or genius, depending on whom you supported—which I have ever seen on a field.

'It's time, three minutes over, blow your bloody whistle, Eric,' came the cry from the Hull bench as their coach Colin Hutton strained to leap on to the field and hug his victorious players.

'Play on. Play on,' came back the call from referee Eric Clay.

Known as the Sergeant-Major, Eric was having no one tell him when to stop the game. But the game would soon be stopped and as play hovered round the half-way line with St. Helens in possession and Hull K.R. prepared to tackle bull-dozers it was all up for another year.

'Give it here, give it here,' screamed Alec, standing deep behind his forwards.

Suddenly the ball was kicked high up field, soaring deep into the Hull territory, high over the heads of everyone—a last-ditch attempt at an 'up an under'. Beneath it on the dead-ball line waited the chunky figure of Cyril Kellett, the Hull K.R. full-back, the heels of his boots planted on the white line. If he had missed the ball, or dared to let it bounce, it would have gone dead. But no, fate decreed him to knock the ball down. Amid a mad scramble on the floor as he sought to regain possession up popped Murphy to pounce on the ball and continue sliding down the players' tunnel. Alec disappeared under a mound of players and spectators, hysterical at the score. But was it a score? Was it not a dead ball and well over the line? Referee Eric Clay, who had been taken by surprise and was fully twenty-five yards behind play, was unsighted. He dashed over to the linesman to consult him, while players argued and spectators waited with baited breath. They spoke for what seemed a full minute. Back came Clay to raise his arm in the air—it was a try. But it wasn't. I had arrived immediately behind Alec to see him pounce on the ball as it slid over the dead-ball line, both player and ball continuing to the players' tunnel. I was not arguing, nor was the linesman, who would be offered the freedom of the borough that night.

Len Killeen, our South African winger, calmly kicked the winning goal to make the score 12-10 in our favour. Clay immediately blew the whistle for full-time. We were mobbed as we left the field, but the Hull team, many in tears, were filled with anger at the rough justice and were unable to hide their feelings. The players' bath was no place for relaxing that evening, the mood was tense and it was no pretty sight to see players of the strength of Cliff Watson and Frank Foster eyeing each other through the steam.

'Bloody robbed, you never scored; you're a liar.' Such was the abuse hurled at Alec in the bath.

'Read the result in the *Liverpool Echo*,' chirped the confident Alec. 'We hammered you,' he insisted, as a couple of Hull players were restrained and guided back to their dressing-room. Such had been the drama and the unexpectedness of the result one could expect such temper, but it was the heat of the moment and it would soon pass. But it was not to pass. Under the rules of the Rugby League the top sixteen clubs at the end of the season's fixtures play in a knockout tournament for the Championship Trophy. The pairing of the sides was done on the basis of the top club playing the sixteenth club and the second playing the

49

fifteenth, and so on. The higher club was given ground advantage through to the final on a neutral ground. Within a month, having been successful in two rounds, we were to meet Hull K.R. in the Championship play-off semi-final, again at Knowsley Road, a week before our Cup Final match at Wembley. The 'needle' between players and spectators was fanned by the authorities' insistence that the match should still be played. It was hardly a suitable time for us with Wembleyitis on our minds. The third round of the Cup had been merely an apéritif for what was to be for me the finest and hardest game of rugby I ever enjoyed—a match which lived up to us Northerners' proud boast, 'it's a man's game'.

Most clubs leave their coach at the entrance to the Knowsley Road car park, but not Hull K.R. on this evening. They rode tall, right to the players' entrance, scattering the crowds gathered at the door waiting for complimentary tickets from their friends in the team. I, in the act of leaving two tickets on the door for old schoolfriends, looked on as tiny boys surged to the coach door only to be shepherded away by a tight-lipped player. 'No autographs until after, lads.' The coach, Colin Hutton, wasn't smiling as usual nor did the players appear too pleased as they filed past me and into the dressing-room without a word passing. They meant business and as their kit baskets were unloaded and carried in by two reserves, clad in the team's smart uniform, there was an air of efficiency about.

The crowd round the door, sensing the occasion, anticipated the clash with their usual cries of 'there's nowt for you here tonight, Hull. Tha wants to keep that bloody Foster caged up!' This was a reference to Hull's skipper, Frank Foster, a player noted for his hardness, but also a shrewd captain on the field. The crowd had begun to build up very early and on my arrival at the ground, an hour before the kick-off, the approaches were lined with Hull coaches. Spectators thronged round the young lad selling rosettes at the side of the pavement. Many newspaper critics favoured Hull, thinking that we would have Wembley on our minds, and many of the St. Helens' spectators, though looking for victory, were prepared to fall back on this excuse in the event of defeat. Few realized outside the club that the team for Wembley had not as yet been selected and, with three or four still playing for a place in the side, there would be no let up. The crowd was well over 20,000 and, with the Hull dressing-room remaining locked, we all knew the meaning behind the game. Hull would be out to prove that we had 'robbed' them. Proof would be given before our own supporters that we were imposters at Wembley. The Hull dressing-room barred all comers until referee Bob Appleyard banged on it for the start. Thirteen players emerged, all wearing the same intent and hypnotized look of men out to right a wrong. Their eyes and ears were covered in protective Vaseline, their hands whitened with resin. The St. Helens team followed, looking no less committed, down the dark tunnel into the light and the roars of the crowd.

When play becomes rough during one of Eddie Waring's rugby commentaries on television, he is often heard to remark in his own inimitable style: 'It's all right. They love this you know. The packs of forwards are merely testing each other for the first ten minutes. A softening-up process.' We tested each other and softened each other up for the whole of the first-half as Tyson, Flanagan and Foster of the Hull pack tore into us with a ferocity rarely seen in a match. Little headway could be made as Albert Halsall, Cliff Watson and myself were dumped unceremoniously with sickening thuds on the ground—'There'll be no prisoners today.' Half-backs Tommy Bishop and Bob Prosser weaved and dodged to little effect, except that Bob did not dodge enough and had to retire at half-time with loose teeth.

When we had looked like crumbling, Frank Barrow, at full-back, had stopped the burly Mike Blackmore and centre Brian Wrigglesworth in their last strides to the line. At 4-4, with two goals each from Killeen and Kellett, we held on into the second-half, but with John Warlow concussed by a well-timed upper-cut on the break up of a scrum and Kel Coslett limping badly after a heavy tackle, our prospects did not look rosy. The grit and courage of the players showed through, none of whom would leave the field though in considerable pain. Here was a job to be done. Let's get on with it was our attitude, and slowly we rose again. Here was the spirit and the will which was to win both Cups—money was not the spur. To this day I do not know what our winning bonus was. It was professional pride which was at stake and an immense loyalty to friends, acquaintances and relatives who made up the crowd. The soccer star, having had a drink in his club's 'Executive Club' or '500 Lounge' after a match, climbs into his expensive car in the reserved car park and rides away to his desirable detached residence in the suburbs. He lives and socializes in a world far removed from the club and the average fan. He can have little point of contact or attachment with the town as he moves around the country in his search for 'the contract'. It is the close proximity at work and at home between player and spectator, the similar social attitudes within the town, which gives a Rugby League man such a pride and a need to win.

We needed to win and within thirteen minutes of the start of the second-half we had picked ourselves up off the floor and were leading 14-6. Two tries by Springbok wing Len Killeen had sealed Hull's fate; the first, in the words of Brian Batty of the *Daily Mail*, coming when '...from just inside his own half Tommy Bishop sent non-stop second-row Ray French racing into Hull K.R.'s half. French got out a wonderful one-handed pass to centre Billy Benyon who handed on for Killeen to streak in from thirty-five yards towards the post.' The second came as Frank Foster surged within yards of our try-line and, passing to a man in support, saw Len Killeen bound in to intercept and race away in a great eighty-five-yard run along the touchline to score ten yards inside the corner flag. The game was now well and truly won, but the final taunt to the opposition had to be made. With only seconds remaining we were awarded a penalty kick and, despite my advice to relax and settle for a kick at goal by Killeen, Alec Murphy launched a huge 'up and under' on the luckless Cyril Kellett, but only after he had indicated to the Hull team with a wave of his hand exactly where it would land. With shades of the Cup match filling everyone's minds, every spectator on the ground watched in eager anticipation for the ball to land. Referee Bob Appleyard waited, Cyril Kellett waited, but unfortunately our exuberant full-back, Frankie Barrow, arrived first, having covered fifty yards to get there, and felled Kellett before the ball descended. The game erupted in a flurry of punches and the referee blew time on his whistle to break up the fighting mêlée of a dozen players.

There were no recriminations after this one. Hull had lost. The communal bath was back to its usual self, filled with the sound of laughter from both sides.

'I thought we had you at half-time. I didn't think your pack could come back,' Colin Hutton observed.

'How's John Warlow? What a beauty of a punch. Mike says it wasn't him.'

More laughter.

'Will Kel's leg be okay for next week? Where are you staying in London?' I had had the good fortune to have played in such a hard, yet skilled game. I could relax over a drink with my opponents. I could chat to the spectators in the club lounge, and on Monday morning in school I could still discuss the match with my colleagues in the staff room at break and during a lesson with my pupils. This is Rugby League with its grip on the community and infiltrating every corner of my life. I could not stop it. I encouraged it.

What more could a man want? Only Wembley and the chance to defeat 'th'owd enemy—Wigan'. We had endured a Cup semi-final at Station Road, Swinton, against Dewsbury, equally as nerve-wracking as both of the Hull K.R. matches. I can well remember my thoughts a few weeks earlier on leaving the Dewsbury ground, along with half-back colleague Wilf Smith and 9,000 spectators, after they had triumphed over Huddersfield 8-2. It had been a dull, forward battle in the third round of the cup.

'It'll be easy,' I thought. 'They are far too slow and nowhere near fit enough for a semi-final.'

'We only have to run them around, Ray, they'll have gone by half-time,' remarked Wilf, as both of us, rather smugly, made our way home by car across the Pennines.

How wrong we were. It was the Saints who had nearly 'gone by half-time', as players whom we had cockily written off as a collection of 'no-hopers and has-beens' showed the 1966 team of all-talents what tackling and covering were all about.

Before the Cup rounds had begun, one of the Dewsbury committee had placed a considerable bet at a price of 1000-1 on Dewsbury reaching Wembley and had promised massive rewards to the players. Now, much to their surprise, they were only eighty minutes from the biggest pay packet of their lives. Ordinary players became supermen. None more so than an old Saints' colleague, Mick Sullivan, the ex-Great Britain wing, now fifteen stones and captaining the side from the loose-forward position. He handled his team with great skill and all his accustomed ferocity. We had been shaken by the underdogs and with twenty minutes of the match remaining we were heading for defeat with chaos reigning in our ranks. Dewsbury players hung on like limpets whenever one of us touched the ball. We were forced back, not forward, by the industry of prop-forward Walker who, though weighing 17 st. 7 lb., ran about the field like a greyhound. Against Huddersfield he and his team had looked ponderous, but now they were our equals. There was no way through. The minnows were surging forward, roared on by a crowd who sensed the upset of the year. Bugles, bells and rattles merged into the crowd's roars. We were about to go under when Len Killeen, ever the master of the unexpected, intercepted a loose pass near our line, swerved away past the tackles and placed the ball behind the Dewsbury posts ninety-five yards away. When he tacked on the goal the Dewsbury morale collapsed, and we were home. Killeen had the nerve to score again and we ran out lucky winners 12-5 but not before I had been involved in a controversial incident with my old friend Mick Sullivan.

The minutes were ticking away and we were content to retain possession and play the game towards the touch-lines when Mick, charging in, hit his head on my raised knee. He dropped to the ground unconscious and with vociferous spectators from the ringside seats swelling over the touch-line and mingling with the scuffling players, Mick was stretchered off, down the tunnel and out of the Challenge Cup.

'That bloody French again with his knees. Get him!' screamed the Dewsbury fans.

I was a marked man but before I could be 'got' the whistle

had blown and I was off to see how Mick was faring in the medical room. He was still unconscious and being attended by the doctor. He had given everything in the game and the knock had finally drained him of his strength. He returned to Dewsbury by car in a semi-conscious state, but there were no hard feelings for he was too good a professional to be bothered.

That was League rugby as I had come to know it—no quarter given, but no personal animosities; hard knocks, but no hard feelings; total commitment to winning, but total respect for opponents and the game.

6
The Wembley Way

There is excitement and effort enough in the routine matches of the League programme. But the adrenalin flows faster for those special games which are the highlight of the year for player and spectator alike. This shared and spontaneous enthusiasm can be evoked by cup matches or by those local encounters which involve whole towns in the tensions of the day. That is why Boxing Day and Good Friday traditionally provide a most effective barometer of Rugby League's welfare. If the annual clashes of St. Helens v Wigan on those days cannot fill the stadiums then nothing can. The rivalry is intense, the action is usually nail-biting and no player can afford to over-indulge in the festivities when he knows that the Wigan match is to be played next day before a 30,000 crowd. Such crowds are commonplace at these games and in the past, as in the second round of the Cup in 1965, they had to be all-ticket affairs to cater for a 45,000 gate. Both teams are the glamour clubs of the League game, both having enjoyed long periods of success, and the rivalry is at its most intense when their fortunes are riding high simultaneously as in the 1960s and early seventies. The crowds are attracted not only by the competition but by the fact that St. Helens and Wigan are two of the game's biggest spenders, pursuing a policy of attracting the best players from League and Union. Each club competes with the other for a precious signature on a League registration form.

Wigan, despite being famed for creating their own local stars in the shape of players such as Ken Gee, Joe Egan and Brian McTigue, have never been afraid to gamble and, like St. Helens, their purchases have always bordered on the spectacular. Tom Van Vollenhoven, Jan Prinsloo, Len Killeen and Ted Brophy were all smart signings from South Africa for St. Helens, but Wigan, too, in the purchase of Fred 'Punchy' Griffiths, Trevor Lake and the ex-Springbok captain and scrum-half Tommy Gentles, also ventured into South Africa with considerable success. Although Tommy Gentles proved to be far too small and light for the game, 'Punchy' Griffiths became a crack goal-kicker and full-back, rescuing the club on many occasions, while Trevor Lake figured in some fine tries on the wing and was a danger to us in the 1966 Cup Final. Wigan's signings of Scotsman George Fairbairn and the New Zealand Maori forward Kurt Sorenson have maintained their tradition, but the most celebrated signing must surely have been Billy Boston, the Cardiff wing, who was to be the counter attraction to our own Tom Van Vollenhoven.

'Voll' was an extraordinary wing, averaging fifty to sixty tries per season at his peak, who appeared to ghost round his opponents by his clever change of pace or sheer speed. He always seemed capable of getting to the try-line even when faced with three or four would-be tacklers. Possessing a fine hand-off, he was immensely strong in the legs and could ride out of tackles before taking off on his long eighty-yard runs with all the grace of a supreme athlete. Boston, or 'Billy B' as he was known to the fans, was different. Signed in 1954 as a youngster from Wales, he became a sensation in the game. Within twelve months he had broken the record for an Australian tour in scoring thirty-six tries and at the end of his career he held the Wigan club's try-scoring record of 475 tries. At fifteen stones he was a fearsome sight coming at you, and in facing a man who could sidestep, swerve, and hand-off, we were often at a loss as to how to stop him. Very often he just powered his way through us and seemed to delight in leaving bodies scattered in his wake. He was an excellent tackler and many centres felt the full impact of his massive bulk when he came in from the wing to take the centre and stop a promising movement. He was the complete footballer and, for all his hardness on the field, was the perfect gentleman off it. Teams would plan their strategies round stopping the likes of 'Billy B' and 'The Voll', and we at St. Helens were no exception, but often with disastrous results in the case of Boston.

I can well remember the planning which went into the attempted stopping of Wigan's famous right-wing pair Eric

Ashton and Billy Boston on one cold Boxing Day clash. Along with Billy Major, then our loose-forward, I had arranged to break quickly from the scrum and go up into the Wigan line and take Boston while Major fell back deep to the touch-line and took Eric Ashton whenever the pair tried their dummy scissors move.

'Billy's calling for the ball, Ray. Break quickly and get up on him when he comes inside,' Billy Major whispered as he packed down behind me in the scrum. 'Let him have it if you catch him.'

'Fair enough,' I replied.

'I'll follow Ashton,' insisted Major.

Wigan duly won the ball from the scrum and up I went to try to stop Boston about to steam inside from Eric Ashton's reverse pass. Disaster struck, for Billy Major somehow got caught up with Eric Ashton as he sped for the touch-line in front of Boston, while I, seeing Boston in my sights, let go with my right arm in the direction of his head. Boston ducked and grinned. Up popped Billy Major to receive the blow intended for Boston. Boston crashed through; Major was led from the field, blood streaming from a cut eye, with the retort: 'Forget the move, Ray, concentrate on the scrum-half.'

Such stars and rivalry were bound to provide the perfect setting for the Wembley Final of May 1966 and it was no surprise at League headquarters that they were able to put up the 'House Full' notices on their first-ever 100,000 gate. For some weeks prior to the match, tickets were only available on the black market and for the first time ticket touts were able to ask exorbitant prices from the fans from the North who were 'up for t'cup'. Such a match elevates the game and the players. Television and the press give it national and world-wide coverage and the excitement which surrounds the build-up makes it a pleasant diversion from the routine round of league games. Many clubs treat the Final as just another match, preferring to train at home and not expose the players to a different environment. But I fail to see how anyone, in the week before, can look at it as a normal match. I think that the atmosphere must be built up —the player must be given the feeling that his talents will be seen by millions throughout the world and he must be made to see it as a special effort. For these reasons I feel that St. Helens' decision to have a week by the seaside at Southport before the match was correct. Such a diversion comes as a necessary break from the normal everyday pressures on players who, after all, are only part-time. For me particularly, it was a welcome rest from the wailing and nightly howls of my baby daughter, Susan, who cried so much that I had been forced to sleep at my mother's house on the night before the previous Cup rounds.

Staying at the Grand Hotel on the seafront at Southport was no idle luxury, and certainly few buckets and spades were taken on the sand dunes at the back of the hotel. Joe Coan maintained his rigorous training to the last, and after a warm-up and tactical sessions on the hotel lawns, I soon got to know every grain of sand on Ainsdale beach, where we pounded up one dune after another. Joe, nicknamed 'Percy Cerutty' after the Australian coach who trained the Olympic athlete Herb Elliott by similar methods, relished the task. He managed to find some mountainous dunes on which he proceeded to have his own mini-Olympics, only with us running in every heat. Tactical planning was held on the lush green turf of the King George VI School playing-fields where we spent many sessions indulging in moves up and down the field, much to the delight of the pupils who flocked to the fields at break and lunch-time. To train with no thoughts or worries of work is ideal, but the most beneficial effect of taking a team away is that it concentrates the whole party on the objective of winning the trophy and helps develop the team spirit which is so necessary. Characters and comedians abound in such conditions and we were certainly not without them in our team whenever we relaxed. For, once the training was done, we looked upon the whole exercise as a holiday. There was no curfew for the players, no petty restrictions. An intelligent team, if it is to have any success, must discipline itself and no amount of external discipline will compensate for wayward characters. Joe Coan knew this and gave the players his trust which I believe was returned both at Southport and in the match itself. At night we entered and left the hotel as we pleased and at dinner we ate and drank what we wanted though it was not always the sedate affair which the Grand Hotel envisaged.

As it was out of the holiday season there were few in the hotel other than the Saints' party, yet every dinner was still taken in grand style in the huge chandeliered ballroom to the accompaniment of a trio whose music resembled the Palm Court orchestra of the thirties. The setting was so Victorian, with unsmiling waiters in immaculate white aprons gliding to and for across the highly polished floor. The only light relief came when the trio tried to dispense with the 'Blue Danube' and, at Albert Halsall's request, to grapple with the unfamiliar notes of 'Hot Diggity'. To enliven the proceedings one evening I arrived late on the ballroom floor from behind a screen, suitably placed in the centre by my make-up artist Cliff Watson. I was clad in an assortment of plastic flowers borrowed from the plant pots in the foyer and two silk scarves from the receptionist. With the trio at last coming to life, we went through a natty little routine to the tune of 'The Stripper'. Thunderous applause ensued when I took a final bow wearing only a daring petal-bedecked jockstrap. Cries of 'More! More!' came from behind and I was shocked to find that, unknown to myself, a coach party of pensioners had trooped into the room thinking that I was part of the cabaret. I had truly given them the bird. It was all good fun and no cause for complaint. One evening, it was I who had cause to complain at live-wire Frankie Barrow when we were trying our luck in the casino with our revolutionary system syndicated by yours truly. The syndicate and system had gone well; we were only losing £22 by ten o'clock. Bob Dagnall, on receiving a cup of coffee and sandwiches which were being given freely by waitresses, was heard to remark: 'Free? It's the dearest cheese butty I've ever had.'

However, with the start of the cabaret, Frankie Barrow turned to nudge my arm as I, full of delusions of grandeur, was vainly clinging to the system.

'Look at that,' he urged, as his attention was directed to the shapely form of Stella Starr, a singer who had arrived on stage.

'Oh it'll do you no good, Frankie. Stick to the cheese butties,' said Bob.

'Rien ne va plus. No more bets,' barked the croupier. 'Eight pays.'

'We've won: £36 to us,' I called and leapt up, only to realize that having diligently placed our bets for the past three hours I had not done so on account of Stella Starr's charms. 'You blasted fool, Frankie.'

'It was your fault, Ray.'

'It wasn't.'

That was the end of the system. Bob called for more butties and coffee, and it was possibly a good thing, too, for I doubt if even our Wembley bonus could have stood the strain of our syndicate.

Any player is too modest for comfort who says that he does not have a sense of his own importance as the coach makes its way along Wembley Way with the supporters waving and pointing their fingers at the window: 'There's Murphy, that's French and Sayer.' The importance of the occasion excites a player when he nears the stadium and I was no exception. 'Will we do it, Ray?' 'Come on the Saints!' Earnest faces peeping from a mass of red and white regalia gazed at us as we alighted from the coach at the entrance to the impressive stadium. A brisk walk through the thronging crowds, a passing handshake, a quick, nervous chat with a couple of friends from London, whom I had known in my Leeds University days, and I was swallowed by the stadium doors. On entering the large and spacious dressing-rooms, I was filled with a sense of awe at the thought of the famous names in all sports who had changed on the very spot. In most dressing-rooms a full team and its reserves makes for a crowded and uncomfortable hour, but here the room was so big that our shoulders barely touched and we could have lain down for a nap if necessary. Arriving early at the ground I needed something to occupy my mind and so I spent an interesting ten minutes inspecting every conceivable medication, liniment, drink, bandage and chewing gum available, all of which were placed neatly by the Wembley authorities on a table alongside the entrance.

'They must be expecting a bloody death,' quipped Tommy

Bishop.

'They think it's the soccer Cup Final,' observed our physiotherapist.

Few spectators appreciate the expert management of a Wembley occasion behind the scenes and the precision timing with which everything takes place. Before being sucked into the 'Wembley time machine' we still had time to tread the famous turf, although a cardboard box containing green sawdust for covering any bare patch from the peering eye of the television cameras tended to detract a little from the image. To come out on to the pitch at Wembley is like emerging from a dark cave into brilliant sunshine and it is necessary to adjust to the light, which, because of the light colour surrounds, can be blinding. I strolled about the pitch and waved to spectators in the stands, at the same time trying to hide a trickle of tears coming down my cheeks.

'I daren't let anyone see me now,' I thought, 'I'm supposed to be the calm and cool member of the team, completely unemotional. That's a laugh.'

I was certainly unnerved at the vast size of the stadium but the 100,000 spectators filled me with no fears. Such a crowd can make a deafening roar, but at Wembley, because of the outside track, the people are so far away from the field they seem impersonal. They appear merely as a sea of faces. I would much rather play before a crowd like this, conscious of no one, than play before twenty or thirty spectators when every shout and sarcastic comment can be heard.

After ten minutes it was back down the dark of the tunnel to the dressing-room where Walter, our skip man, had hung the thirteen new red and white shirts on the pegs.

'New shorts, new stockings, new jerseys displaying proudly the town's crest on the front...Walter couldn't have...?' I thought. 'No he hasn't.'

It was there, the same jock strap I had used with loving care since he had handed it to me on my first training session. Wembley would not be the same without it. We were soon ready for the last-minute comments of Joe Coan, the coach, but by now I was concentrating on tuning myself for the kick-off and only took in his last words: 'Run them about.

They're a team of old men.' Following the customary handshakes among team-mates and directors we filed into the huge tunnel and approach to the pitch, each team coming nervously from its dressing-room, one on each side of the tunnel at exactly the same time. With the strains of 'Abide with Me' filtering down to the players, I made a last check to pass the time. Shorts cord not too tight? Can't stop fingers adjusting the shoulder pads. I tried a nervous joke to Laurie Gilfedder, the Wigan second-row, lined up alongside me. This is a most awkward time next to your opponent, wishing him, 'the best of luck', asking him, 'are you okay?' when really you do not mean it. I was more concerned about the man with the stopwatch, waiting for him to signal the processional walk to the centre of the field to shake hands with the then Prime Minister, Harold Wilson.

'The walk is timed for two minutes, so don't dawdle.' Such were the instructions given by the small man in the white coat.

During the walk I could not help laughing at Tommy Bishop waving frantically at people in the stands. 'He must have bought tickets for everyone in the street,' I commented to John Mantle who made up the rear of the Saints' column of players, all walking behind our proud chairman, Harry Cook. 'I wonder who'll get the biggest cheer when the players file off after their names are called over the tannoy?'

'Must be Murph or Voll, second-rows and loose-forwards hardly raise a shout. The crowds are a spent force by then.'

They were still roaring their appreciation when the forwards' names came over the loudspeakers: 'Watson, Sayer, Halsall, Warlow...' the voice boomed with its southern accent, so foreign at the Northerners' day out. 'French.' I was jolted into action and strode to our side of the pitch, impatient to get started. And before I knew where I was the match had started at three o'clock, not a second too soon and not a second too late.

A classic struggle had been anticipated by the press, and the crowd settled down expecting a magnificent showpiece of open rugby which such players could easily produce. It was not to be. We were concerned with winning, not entertaining, and as I received the ball from the kick-off we settled into a pattern of play heavily reliant on our strong pack which had carried all before it that season. I was dumped unceremoniously on the turf by huge prop Danny Gardiner, his face full of venom. I knew we were in for a battle with no quarter given or asked. Controversy had surrounded the final, for Wigan's normal hooker, Colin Clarke, had been suspended in the previous week and, in desperation, they had been forced to play a local lad, Tom Woosey, who, being a solid prop, had little experience of hooking. Against our experienced and wily old campaigner, international Bill Sayer, ironically signed from Wigan only four months before, the Wigan pack failed to gain their accustomed share of possession. We were therefore given the freedom of the field and, supremely confident of regaining the ball at the breakdown, we swept downfield in close forward play. This abundance of possession enabled us to hover in the Wigan half in the opening quarter and, though Wigan's fine cover defence, led by Harry Major and Tony Stephens, held out, we were awarded two kicks at goal. The first one Len Killeen put over from a straightforward position but his second goal was, I believe, the crucial factor in our winning the Cup, not for its two points, but for its effect on morale.

We were awarded a fairly innocuous penalty about sixty yards from the Wigan line and Len came in from the wing, as he thought, to place the ball into touch deep into the Wigan half. Play was on the touch-line and, with Alec Murphy our captain at centre on the opposite touch-line, I gave orders for Len to kick at goal. He stared at me in disbelief, looking at the posts far away in the distance.

'No chance,' he chortled, 'I'll put it in touch.'

'Have a go, Len. If you miss it we will still be on their line.'

My idea was not that he would kick the goal, but, knowing the power of Len's boot, I wanted to keep Wigan on their own line in the early stages of the game. We stood arguing for half a minute until Alec came up.

'Get the bloody goal kicked, Lennie,' he snapped, having the same intention as me.

Len cheekily teed up the ball amid gasps from the crowd who could hardly believe the attempt. Eric Ashton could be heard staking his players in a defensive situation near the posts obviously expecting the ball to drop short. Few expected Len to kick it. But he did. He placed the ball firmly and high between the posts to register one of the most incredible goals ever seen at Wembley. We were winning 4-0 inside ten minutes, but more important was the feeling within the side, admirably summed up by our full-back Frankie Barrow on his way to the restart, 'It's ours, lads, we can't go wrong. Get into them, lads.'

'Get into them' we did and oozing confidence we went further ahead when Tommy Bishop and Albert Halsall swept the ball through Peter Harvey to Tom Van Vollenhoven. Tom slipped a good pass inside to John Mantle who was backing up and, handing-off a Wigan defender, he crashed over near the touch-line. Killeen tacked on the goal, by now relishing his kicks like a star at the Royal Command Performance. We could not stop him kicking.

Wigan, encouraged by two points from a Laurie Gilfedder goal, hit back hard and I vividly recall the only moment in the match, when a couple of minutes before half-time, I felt the game could slip away. Before the match I had heard so much about the energy-sapping qualities of the Wembley turf. I had heard of players being drained at half-time, and I must confess I had never believed it, for I looked upon it as merely another pitch covered with the same green grass as Knowsley Road, St. Helens. Yet when I had to cross the field for about forty yards to a scrummage near our line I suddenly felt as if I had no legs. I was weak. I trailed last to the pack, delaying the time, looking at the hands on the clock. 'If Sos doesn't hook this ball, I'm done,' I thought.

I leaned in the scrum for what appeared to be an eternity when suddenly the ball was beneath my eyes in the second-row. Tommy Bishop snapped it up and ran it out towards the blind side of the pack. Cliff Watson took it once, John Warlow took it a second time, while I could only look on. The whistle went for half-time.

'We've won it. Thanks Sos.'

We did just that in the second-half, for though Wigan gained a greater share of the ball from the scrums there was no suppressing our eagerness. An ageing Wigan side began to tire rapidly, allowing gaps for the likes of Billy Benyon and Peter Harvey to create more chances for maestro Len Killeen, who added a try and a penalty goal within ten minutes of the restart. A further try from Tommy Bishop, a conversion from Len again, who by now was well on the way to the award of the Lance Todd Trophy for the player of the Final, and Wigan were a spent team. They knew it for Brian McTigue had tried every trick to rouse his pack and it had been beaten. Eric Ashton and Billy Boston had received only few chances, being starved of the ball, but it was left to mercurial Murphy to put the finishing touches on the show with an outrageous drop-goal two minutes before time when the score stood at 19-2. Ever controversial, after the match, Alec was bitterly accused of gamesmanship and illegal tactics by the press (particularly in Wigan) for frequently going off-side. His supposed ploy had been to make Wigan kick for touch at the resultant infringement and therefore give the Saints the chance of winning the ball from the scrums. He is supposed to have ruined the game as a spectacle, but the only people he ruined it for were from Wigan. I can honestly say that as pack leader I never heard of such tactics nor did he ever indicate any to me. Close scrutiny of the film of the match will show that he was off-side on very few occasions and certainly on nothing like the number attributed to him by the press. Wigan had been unable to last the pace. We had trained hard, we were fit, and once in the lead in the early stages it is amazing how much fitter we became.

The Cup was ours, and we climbed the steps to the dignitaries' box where Harold Wilson duly presented it to Alec Murphy before the team's ceremonial lap of honour round the pitch. I must confess to disliking this practice, feeling that there is no need for such adulation of professional players. We had been paid to do a job. We had done it and it was now time to leave the stage. I felt embarrassed at the thought and, intending no disrespect to our fans, I calmly walked with our skip man across the pitch to meet the lads at the approach to the tunnel for the endless inane television interviews and rather ludicrous 'talk me through the try' routines.

'How did you feel when you scored that try?'

'I... er... felt... er... great... er... it was... er... great.'

It was over and it was won. I felt sorry for the losers trooping down the tunnel with heads bent low. However, Saturday night was no place for tears, as, re-united with our wives, we attended the reception. Following this we went on to the bright lights of London to celebrate at a Mayfair night club—only to receive a bill, for six halves of beer and six drinks for the wives, of £15.

'I'm not paying that,' I announced and was promptly asked if I would mind stepping out into the foyer where the manager would like a word with me.

'What's the trouble?' the manager asked.

'I'm not paying £1 for a glass of beer,' I explained.

'I see,' said the manager.

At this point it became obvious that the atmosphere had become distinctly chilly and that several large gentlemen standing round were bouncers about to be invited by the manager to earn their keep for the evening.

'Hold on a minute,' I said. I went back inside the club and said to the rest of the Saints' forwards, 'Follow me.'

Back in the foyer the manager surveyed the Saints' pack and then his bouncers and was not long in making up his mind. 'I think, gentlemen, that you had better have this round of drinks on the house.'

We did, then left. It had been our day all round. And as we laughed and sang our way home there was no premonition that soon I would be bounced out of a much more important club.

7
Recharged by Widnes

It was pride which started me in League rugby. And it was hurt pride which spurred me to my finest personal achievement in the League game. The shock of being bartered away by St. Helens like some worn-out car roused me to new endeavour and gave my rugby career the new stimulus it needed.

I had rarely given a thought to the possibility of leaving my home town club, particularly when for the season 1966/67 I was made captain, on Alex Murphy's departure to Leigh. Although we figured in yet another Championship Final that season against Wakefield Trinity, we also saw the break up of the successful Wembley side. In August 1967, I was involved in a part-exchange deal which took the Widnes captain Frank Myler to St. Helens and me to Widnes. For both of us it was to be a new lease of life as players, but I did not realize this when I received a telephone call from Basil Lowe, the Saints' secretary. He asked me to come up to the club where it was quickly made obvious that I had little part in the St. Helens team of the future, and that a couple of the Widnes committee were coming to see me that afternoon. Aged twenty-eight and captain of the foremost club in Rugby League, I had looked forward to at least four more seasons of personal and team success at St. Helens. I was most hurt at the thought that I was no longer to play a part in that future. I had captained the side through the difficult period following the successes of the 1965/66 season and had steadied the reins sufficiently for the side to be still ranked as one of the strongest, despite losing match-winners of the calibre of Alec Murphy, Albert Halsall and Len Killeen. I felt that my best rugby was still to come; now I was to be discarded. I still had a pride in my performances and in those of the team. It was a shock to me, and I freely admit that I felt a great sense of grievance, as I listened to the committees of both clubs who viewed the transfer on a

68

most impersonal basis.

'We want a centre, Frank Myler, and Widnes will not part unless they have you as their captain and pack leader.'

'What if I don't want to go?'

'Then there's no deal. It's all off,' chipped in Harry Cook the chairman.

But the atmosphere was such that if I had not agreed to the situation it would have been 'all off' for Ray French at St. Helens. This was the harsh, brutal side of the game where players, with or without their wishes, are bartered and traded as goods on a supermarket shelf. I felt like a piece of meat which had not yet gone bad, but which was being sold at the right price at the right time before it went 'off'. I was expected by the Saints' directors to go 'off', but, thanks to Widnes, the next four years were to be among the most successful of my career.

However, if anyone had asked me for my opinions of life at Widnes a month after my arrival, I would have described the situation with despair, because the club was in complete contrast to the professionalism of the Saints. The attitude was far too relaxed, particularly in the approach to the game by many of the younger players who seemed to look upon the matches as an excuse to earn a little beer money; nobody minded unduly about defeat. There were too few 'professionally-minded' players, while the committee were at fault for condoning an easy-going attitude. I believe it was Vince Karalius, on his return to Widnes in 1972, who brought the club up to the professional demands of the game, with the result that Widnes now rank among the most successful of all clubs, and have a highly competent committee, most thorough in their approach to Rugby League. My opinions, though, changed rapidly, for no newcomer could fail to be impressed by the enthusiasm and dedication to the club of men such as Tommy Shannon and Frank Tobin, surely one of sport's best physiotherapists, and the concern for the welfare of the players shown by the committee. The majority of the players were young, many I had taught and coached as a schoolmaster in Widnes years earlier, and many of these youngsters—John Foran, George Nicholls, Keith Elwell, Reg Bowden, Mal Aspey and Eric Hughes—were later to play a prominent part in Widnes's three successive Wembley finals in 1975, 1976 and 1977. Players such as Nicholls and Elwell also toured Australia. It was a pleasure to play with these lads and I like to think that I had some part in their eventual success. Certainly they helped my play.

As captain I was in a position of complete control both on and off the field, an arrangement which suited me admirably, and I was able to play the game as I wanted and not as I was directed. Many would comment on the change in my own play from my period at St. Helens, where I had the role of a grafting, tackling forward, an accompaniment to the running of Dick Huddart and John Mantle. At Widnes I had to do all the ball carrying and most of the passing for the younger ones to run on to, a style of play which I enjoyed and which proved much more effective in my quest for League honours. The atmosphere in the club was a happy, carefree one and I rarely felt the pressures which I had experienced at St. Helens. Defeat brought few recriminations. As a team we lacked consistency, but proved more than a match on many occasions for the likes of Saints, Wigan and Salford where our spirit and keenness made up for our deficiencies. For a team to maintain the consistency which is needed to win cups and championships, they must have a sufficient number of older, experienced players who can play to a high level throughout the season yet raise their performance for the most important matches. In doing so they encourage the younger ones to play better in every match.

Our Widnes team in my few seasons with them lacked a sufficient number of mature players, and though the players could raise their level for matches against St. Helens and Wigan, in fact beating them on more occasions than they beat us, we often slumped to the likes of Barrow, Whitehaven and Leigh. I have stressed the need for good players to play with good teams if they are to reach their full potential, and at Widnes I did have players alongside me who did just that while others, equally good, did not reach the heights of which they were capable. Two half-backs, Jimmy Boylan and Dennis O'Neill, in the years 1967 to 1970, were for me a combination equal to any I have ever played with. Jimmy Boylan was a crafty and skilful scrum-half who probably won the man-of-the-match award at Widnes more often than any other player. He could invariably make something out of nothing, even behind a beaten pack. Dennis O'Neill in these years was possibly the fastest stand-off playing in League, with tremendous acceleration away from the scrums. Some of his spectacular tries lit up many a gloomy Saturday afternoon at Widnes. Unfortunately Jimmy became somewhat disillusioned at our lack of success, while Dennis, though a sound player and admirable servant to the club over the past seasons, suffered a long spate of injuries which would have quenched anyone else's spirit. Both players with the right club at the right time would have been ranked with the highest. Of those younger players who did come good none was more successful than Ray Dutton, who remained with the club through its glorious seasons of the seventies and proved to be a fine international full-back and a grand club servant. George Nicholls, my eager young second-row partner of those days, was one player who moved to St. Helens, where he became the top second-row in the game and was to feature in World Cup and Great Britain teams abroad. George was destined for success for he would listen to everything that was said to him. He watched other players and was one of the most willing of forwards when it came to the hard graft. He blossomed into a fine example of the strong-tackling and hard-running player, my ideal for a second-row in Rugby League.

The Widnes-born lad never lacks grit or honest application —he brings a fine spirit to Rugby League. But the days have gone when any team could be built on, say, thirteen Widnes- or St. Helens-born players. No matter what talent these areas produce, a side must be more cosmopolitan, the horizons must be broader, for the player from outside can bring many new ideas on play and at the same time absorb the qualities from the locals. This has been the successful policy at St. Helens for years, to blend local-born and imported players, and to my mind this is also the key to Widnes's recent successes. Their signings of John Warlow, Jim Mills, Doug Laughton and Ken Gill (all highly experienced League internationals) coupled with Union men of the calibre of Glyn Shaw of Wales have proved the worth

71

of the policy.

My memories of matches at Widnes are therefore of games of peaks and lows. The high points include the excellent wins, as at Featherstone in 1968 in the Rugby League Challenge Cup when, in a sea of mud, we defeated one of the most powerful of teams on their own ground. But my unhappiest memory is of a defeat by Leigh a couple of years later, again in the Challenge Cup, when Alec Murphy produced a trick from the bag equal to his tricks on my behalf against Hull K.R. Leading Leigh in the last seconds of the match we were sorely pressed a yard from our line and under our posts when the referee blew for a scrum. This decision did not look too serious for us, as our hooker was winning a lot of the ball. However, I had reckoned without Alec Murphy, for with the referee rapidly losing patience at his attempts to put the ball into the scrum, Alec merely bounced it off his own prop's bottom, snapped the ball up and set up a try near the posts before anyone could object, least of all the referee. No one had moved, the ball had never been in the scrum, but he had got away with it. Only Alec could have managed this. I 'played hell' with him but Alec merely shrugged his shoulders and roared with laughter. He had won and we had lost. He moved on to even greater heights when he led Leigh to the trophy at Wembley. For Widnes there were only the thoughts of what might have been, and for me an even higher estimation of Alec's ability and cheek.

Personally, the most interesting clashes were with my old club St. Helens, and how well I can remember the pleasure which our wins against them gave me. It was reminiscent of the old-time gunfighter who feels his time is not yet up, though some would consign him prematurely to Boot Hill. The gunfighter still feels he has a point to prove. I think I proved more than a point in our wins against the Saints over the next four seasons but, paradoxically, it was a defeat that gave me the greatest satisfaction when we lost 13-18 to St. Helens in March 1968 and I was made man of the match. The game was one of two halves with Widnes leading by thirteen points just before half-time, only to be overhauled two minutes before full-time. The match produced six tries for the wings, three to each side, surely a rare occurrence in the game. Tom Ashcroft, the local St. Helens rugby writer, summed up my play: 'We had him as the tactical kicker to touch, the undisputed pack leader and an example to all by his ability to get the pass away as he was being submerged in the tackle.' (The phrase 'tactical kicker' I treasure, for on the only other occasion on which I kicked a ball I attempted to place a grubber kick for Tom Van Vollenhoven near an opponent's line. The kick was too short and the opposite wing scooped up the ball and scored at the other end of the pitch, fully ninety yards away. I had to troop back to the line to the accompaniment of some choice comments from our spectators.) Such is the atmosphere in a match when a transferred player returns to his former club that it makes for a stronger edge to his game, but his old friendships are still maintained afterwards.

In victory or defeat the dressing-room at Widnes was always full of humour, welcoming a long succession of local, talented, schoolboy League players and the occasional Union convert. Most Union converts in those days were from the local Union clubs and settled in well, though we did have some trouble in accommodating one, Jim Fitzpatrick, in his first game. Not even Tommy Shannon, the ever-dependable skip man, bargained for Big Jim's feet when he searched frantically for a pair of size 12 boots twenty minutes before a television floodlit trophy match was due to kick off. None could be found and the only solution was a pair of 10½s loosely tied and soaked in a bucket of water. Imagine the touch judge's surprise when he came into the Widnes dressing-room that night to see Big Jim, five minutes before the kick-off, sitting with his feet in a bucket of water. Prepared for the worst, Jim took to the field and proceeded to have a very effective first twenty minutes of Rugby League. As the game wore on and we were pressed back in our own half, I noticed him about twenty yards behind play, but I thought this was due to his inexperience. I looked again a little later, and Jim was still there.

'My boots, Ray, I can't move. I think they've shrunk.'

Few captains can have been faced with such a situation in the heat of the game. There was only one thing to do. I passed the ball to him and called, 'Stay down in the tackle.'

Jim gratefully did, and after urgent promptings to the bench was mercifully substituted and hobbled from the field, his face in contortions, to rid himself of his boots.

Such was the humour in the club, and as I relaxed in my play so my personal fortunes soared. With St. Helens I had been part of a magnificent team which collectively had won every medal, cup and honour it was possible to win. At Widnes, collectively we won few honours, but there I was to achieve the ambition of every player—a trip to Australia and New Zealand as a World Cup player in the summer of 1968. This followed my selection as Lancashire captain and two games for Great Britain against France. My only regret is that what should have been a side easily good enough to win the World Cup failed to do so through a combination of ill luck and ill judgement. For all of us involved, the winning was much more important than the taking part—but what an experience it was, even in defeat.

8
The Lost World

Selection for the World Cup was a heady experience and there was much to sharpen the anticipation of what lay ahead. Before we left Manchester airport on Saturday 18 May 1968 on the first stage to Sydney, Australia, we had undergone perhaps the most thorough preparations of any League team journeying abroad. Training sessions had been held during the season for a large body of players from whom the tour party was to be chosen. These sessions were arranged at various grounds in Lancashire and Yorkshire under the guidance of the genial Colin Hutton, a coach of long-standing reputation, who used the sessions to build up a team spirit and friendly atmosphere among the players. The further provision of games against selected sides—Leeds, Salford and Halifax—was certainly a fine chance for the party to mould together and to try out any moves or tactics for the weeks in Australia. This insistence on practice games has rarely been tried in League, but it certainly has much to commend it, for in our three wins against the clubs, we gained in confidence and developed a knowledge of each other's play. With such thorough planning, our chances of knocking the Aussies from their pedestal looked rosy.

However, our hopes took a serious blow when the prospective captain, Neil Fox of Wakefield Trinity, had to withdraw from the squad with a serious injury, leaving me to act as captain in the Salford and Halifax games. I must admit immediately to a biased opinion here, for I certainly hoped for the captaincy. Having performed well in both trial games and been complimented by the pressmen for my leadership, I was naturally disappointed to be passed over in preference to Bev Risman, the Leeds full-back. And while I do not think that I or Tommy Bishop, my next choice, would have been better captains, that appointment set a tone for the tour which, in my opinion, was misguided.

Bev has been a very good friend of mine throughout our Union and League careers and I would certainly rate him as an exceptionally talented player, who at the time of the World Cup series, was the best equipped full-back for the trip. However, I fear that he lacked the dynamic personality to captain a side in Australia. A quiet and modest player off the field, Bev lacked the strong, dominant, even nasty streak needed in Australia, where a captain must dictate and take bold steps both on and off the field. Without the responsibility, Bev would have been a fine attribute to any touring side, but I am sure that his own form began to suffer with the many off-the-field activities, so necessary for a skipper to undertake.

All the preparations in England were undone by the planning of the tour itinerary, which scheduled Great Britain to play Australia on the Saturday following our flight from Manchester, to be followed by two further games against New Zealand and France on the successive Saturdays. Following the World Cup tournament we were to remain in Australia for a further two weeks touring in Queensland where we were due to play exhibition matches of little consequence. These matches should have been played prior to the World Cup in order to give the team a period of acclimatization and a chance to adjust to Australian playing styles and conditions. I realize that there would probably have been the risk of injury before the big games took place, but the experience of these matches would have been invaluable to newcomers such as myself. The first game for many of us in Australia was a Test match at the Sydney Cricket Ground, five days after a thirty-four-hour flight. This was hardly the correct preparation for a game of such stature. The party had insufficient time to socialize and live with each other, and insufficient time to recognize each other's faults and qualities. Any touring party, and ours was no exception, will contain players of differing attitudes, all of whom have to be moulded into one unit by the captain and management. We had our quiet ones such as Alan Burwell and Chris Young from Hull K.R. and Derek Edwards of Castleford, and our extrovert, rumbustious characters in Tommy Bishop (St. Helens), Kevin Ashcroft (Leigh) and 'Flash' Flanagan (Hull

K. R.). The nationalities must merge too when a party has Welshmen such as John Warlow and Clive Sullivan, and a Scot with a dry sense of humour in Charlie Renilson, who was to return to Sydney for a spell of playing and coaching following our trip. Solid, honest-to-goodness Englishmen in the shape of Mick Shoebottom, Cliff Watson, and Arnie Morgan helped to mould the party, but it was to take time, and a week was not enough. The social life was hectic in that first week in Sydney and came as a shock to many of us used to the rather sedate atmosphere off the field of a Lancashire or Yorkshire small town. Many of the players, led by an Australian tycoon known affectionately as 'Last Card' Louie (on account of his huge winnings on the turn of a playing card), were introduced to the delights of the 'Pink Pussy Club' and were wined and dined at every opportunity. Above all, even when socializing, the Aussies made no bones about their desire to beat us and inflict disaster on the 'pommy bastards', so that wherever we were there was no escape from the World Cup. In many a bar, club, or restaurant, I played the game many times over with some hard-bitten Aussie poking his finger at me and telling me what a lousy 'pom' I was. He enjoyed it and certainly I did, for, despite all their aggressive attitude which comes out on the sporting field, they are among the most hospitable of people and generous to their visitors to the point of excess.

However, those who have taken part in any sport against the Australians will surely testify to their desire to win and their competitive attitude. Rugby League is no exception. The Australian players' physical prowess coupled with a fanaticism for fitness makes them ideal for the tough, fast-running game of League, particularly that played on their hard grounds. I feel, however, that their players are so obsessed with strength and fitness that many tend to make that their whole game, with the result that Australia has produced few ball-playing forwards—with the exception of the world-class Sydney St. George loose-forward Johnnie Raper. Though exporting many backs—Devery, Cooper and Bevan for example—to English Rugby League, they have had in recent years to resort to importing our forwards such as Brian McTigue, Bill Ashurst and Mal Reilly to teach their

77

packs the ball-playing skills. Nevertheless, most clashes with the Aussies are rough, bruising affairs in which players must stand their ground or go under. Prior to the tour I had played on three occasions against their touring sides, for St. Helens twice, and Widnes once, and had gained a healthy respect for their arrogant play and abrasive attitude. My own attitude towards them was influenced by our controversial international wing, Mick Sullivan, who relished the thought of playing against any Aussie and was not afraid to tell him so. Long before the days of Mohammed Ali and his 'psyching' of opponents, I recall Mick, at a post-match reception in St. Helens Town Hall for our colonial visitors, strolling casually up to Peter Dimond, the tough, brash Aussie wing who, having played against one of our reserves that day, was enjoying himself with the buffet. 'Eh, Dimond. You're playing against me next week in the Test match, not a reserve. Eat a lot, it may be your last.'

Mick meant it and took this attitude to the matches, where he always commanded the respect of the Aussies. Club games such as these whetted my appetite for the tour, but even I was amazed at the strength and wealth of Rugby League in Australia, particularly in Sydney, where the clubs would put many of our soccer clubs in the shade. Financed essentially by rows and rows of 'one-arm bandits', the headquarters of clubs such as Eastern Suburbs, St. George and South Sydney are truly impressive, providing restaurants, swimming pools, night clubs, saunas, lounge bars and so on —one even having a club yacht anchored in Sydney harbour to provide sight-seeing trips for the fans. The clubs are geared to attracting families by providing every conceivable form of entertainment in multi-million-pound complexes which make our own attempts with social clubs at Salford, St. Helens and Warrington look rather small. The wealth generated in these entertainment centres is for the development of rugby and therefore the stars are paid the equal of soccer players in this country. Man-of-the-match awards and player-of-the-season awards command huge sums of money. Sponsorship offers lucrative contracts to the clubs and players to such an extent that British Rugby League has suffered from a spate of transfers in recent seasons which has taken many of our best players to Sydney, seeking fat playing contracts. The game in Australia is at national level and the opportunities are unlimited. For myself, the press and constant publicity surrounding our tour and the League game created an edge to my play. I wanted to be involved. I wanted to beat them. The taunts in the streets and, at the Sydney Cricket Ground during our training, the constant barracking of the watchers with 'You're hopeless, you pommy bastards' was enough to fire anyone with the will to give his all.

Our hotel, the Olympic, overlooked the Cricket Ground with our training area in front. From our balcony, where Cliff Watson, John Warlow, and myself stood, the sight of the stadium and its surrounds on the morning of the match was awe-inspiring and slightly unnerving. The crowds, even at nine o'clock, were streaming to the ground, all carrying their famous 'cooler boxes' which were stocked with cans of ice-cold beer to keep them watered throughout the day. Great Britain v Australia day kick-offs at ten o'clock with a succession of junior and club matches right to the time of the big game. The Aussies settle in the stands or on the notorious 'Hill', usually drinking freely. They are certainly in the right mood for the match by two-thirty. Our hotel, being situated on the corner of the main thoroughfare, was a port of call for spectators and the bars downstairs did roaring trade while we were closeted upstairs for the team talk in the residents' television lounge. Ex-internationals, such as Dick Huddart, called to wish me good luck before we set out on the short walk to the stadium. We had to thread our way through the endless stream of spectators, but I felt that this experience was good tactically on Colin Hutton's part, for the ribald comments and banter of the onlookers put me in the mood for the match. All my thoughts were concentrated on the forthcoming game as I walked, speaking to no one.

On reflection, however, I must confess that for me the game had already been lost by the very selection of the side. Though I was never certain, the selectors seemed to comprise the manager, Bill Fallowfield, the assistant and coach, Colin Hutton, Bev Risman, and the chairman of the Rugby Football League, John Smallwood. Here I believe they were all sadly astray in their ideas and desires to play the Aussies 'at football'. Players who could indulge in all the prettier aspects of rugby were selected to the exclusion of men such as John Warlow and Arnie Morgan in the forwards, two players of rough and uncompromising reputations in England. Our whole attitude to this initial match in the series was misdirected, for we should have met them head on physically in order to undermine their pack's confidence. It was not to be, yet the sight of 62,000 spectators packing the ground, many of whom had camped overnight outside, set the heart fluttering. Their shrieking and shouting over the clatter of the beer cans does something for the spirit.

Our dressing-room beneath the stand was unusually tense when referee John Percival entered to clear up any misunderstanding over the Australian interpretation of the 'play the ball' situation. In a demonstration to Bev Risman, he illustrated his method of placing the ball on the floor before heeling it to the man waiting behind. He was most meticulous in this and, though we listened attentively, it did not stop him from penalizing us at the first instance in the game. Nor did it stop him from penalizing us all through the match to give the Aussie full-back, Eric Simms, the opportunity to kick eight goals. Our rhythm was upset by his constant use of the whistle and, though we scored two tries through Ian Brooke and Clive Sullivan, our pack was not strong enough to contain the forward surges of Artie Beeson, Ron Coote and, above all, Johnny Raper at loose-forward. We indulged in too many moves and too much lateral passing in the early stages with our pack, instead of meeting them in a full-blooded encounter for the first twenty minutes. They surely had expected it from a Great Britain pack. With Tommy Bishop working himself to a frenzy and being booed on every occasion that he touched the ball, we tried in vain to contain the green and gold jerseys, but with the game still evenly poised at the three-quarter stage it was Raper who sealed our fate. With a strong run following a clever dummy pass in midfield he galloped thirty yards to score under the posts, leaving Eric Simms the simplest of conversions. The Australians pulled away as our morale sagged, while Tommy Bishop had a verbal battle with the referee. We lost 10-25 to a stronger

1. The England Rugby Union team 1961.
Back row: M. Weston, P. Wright, J.
Wilcox, D. Morgan, V. Harding, R. French,
Budge Rogers, L. Rimmer. *Front row:*
R. Sharpe, J. Roberts, E. Robinson, R.
Jeeps, R. Jacobs. J. Young, B. Risman.

2.   Wales v England, Cardiff Arms Park,
January 1961. Despite the efforts of Ray
French (second from left), O'Connor
(Wales) manages to keep possession of
the ball in a maul.

3. England v France, Twickenham, February 1961. England's forwards (white shirts) clean up a slippery loose ball at the feet of the French hooker, de Gregorio, who is making a determined challenge.

4. England v France, Twickenham, February 1961. The ball goes loose as Ray French effectively smother-tackles de Gregorio with a bear-like hug. Jeeps, the England captain, is in close attendance.

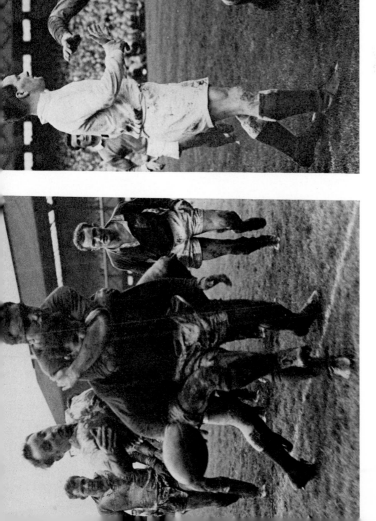

5. England v France, Twickenham, February 1961. Using a wrestler's headlock, French forces Saux into touch.

6. England v France, Twickenham, February 1961. Ray French moves to a quick throw-in at the line but the ball goes loose as Lacroix (dark shirt) is hoisted on to an England player's back.

7. England v France, Twickenham, February 1961. Clever obstruction at the line-out by France's forwards (dark shirts) prevents Harding, jumping at three, and French, at five, from winning the ball.

8. England v Scotland, Twickenham, March 1961. With French in close support, a midfield break by Jeeps is brought to a halt by a solid tackle from Bruce of Scotland.

9. England v Scotland, Twickenham, March 1961. A tussle for a loose ball following a line-out. Ray French, in scrum cap, appears to be wrestling with C. R. Jacobs, England's No. 1

10. Chaired by his team-mates, Vince Karalius, the St. Helens captain, holds the Lancashire Cup after his side had defeated Swinton in the 1962 Final.

11. St. Helens v New Zealand, Knowsley Road, St. Helens, 1961. The determination is there, but French suffers a heavy tackle as he tries to break out of defence.

12. A training-session shortly after French's signing for St. Helens in August 1961. Coach Stan McCormick explains the finer points of forward play to (*l. to r.*) Mike Knowles, Cliff Watson, Ray French and Keith Ashcroft.

13. A triumphant dive by Ray French as he scores the winning try a couple of minutes before full-time in the Western Championship Final against Swinton at Central Park, Wigan, 1964.

14. With the ball tucked firmly under his arm, French makes a determined run at the Hull K.R. defence in the semi-final of the 1966 Championship play-off.

15. Tommy Bishop, confidently perching on Ray French's shoulder, uses a ball to demonstrate how he will hold the cup aloft in a break from training during the build-up to the 1966 Wembley Cup Final.

16. Under the watchful eye of Ray French, Prime Minister Harold Wilson is introduced to John Mantle before the start of the Rugby League Cup Final between St. Helens and Wigan in 1966.

17. Although there is no love lost between two sides during a final, French still has time for a smile after a duel with Wigan's skipper Eric Ashton.

18. With a blessing from a supporter, Alec Murphy, the St. Helens captain, leads his smiling, victorious team back to the pitch after receiving the Rugby League Challenge Cup from Prime Minister Harold Wilson in 1966.

19. Victory is sweet. Murphy holds the cup aloft to show the St. Helens supporters, while delighted team-mates look to find wives, relatives and friends in the crowd.

20. The Great Britain Rugby League side before playing France at the Parc des Princes, Paris, 1968. *Back row:* I. Brooke, C. Renilson, M. Clarke, C. Watson, A Morgan, R. French, J. Warlow, K. Edwards. *Front row:* B. Risman, F. Flanagan, C. Young, R. Millward, N. Fox, T. Bishop, A. Burwell.

21. England v France, Bradford, 1968. Ray French and Ian Brooke look on as Chris Young is firmly tackled.

22. Ray French, seen off for Australia at the airport by his wife in 1968, signs an autograph for the daughter of the Widnes physiotherapist Frank Tobin.

23. Great Britain v Australia, Sydney Cricket Ground, 1968. Cliff Watson, supported by Ray French, drives for the line.

24. The Great Britain tour party in the airport coach on the way from Sydney to Brisbane for the match against Queensland, July 1968. Front seats occupied by (l. to r.) Arnie Morgan (Featherstone Rvrs.), Mick Clarke (Leeds), Chris Young (Hull K.R.) and Clive Sullivan (Hull). Tommy Bishop (St. Helens) (seated behind Chris Young) reads a press report. Ray French is seated behind Bishop.

25. Ray French caught in characteristic pose on the touch-line in a photograph taken by a pupil at Cowley School. (All the action is off camera.)

26. French demonstrates the importance of keeping the eye on the ball as he is put under pressure by one of his young players.

27. French's students listen intently as he explains a point on scrummaging.

28. Teaching boys the basic rugby skills is vital to the game's future. Here French receives a well-delivered pass.

29. The other Ray French in teaching attire at Cowley School.

and more determined side.

After the Australian game, though I was upset at our defeat, I had been well pleased with my own form and was heartened to see that Noel Kelly, that fine ex-Australian skipper, had remarked in his newspaper column: 'Karalius would have wept. I never thought that I'd be wasting my sympathy on any pommy forward, but I couldn't help feeling sorry for their one-man pack Ray French last Saturday. He was crucified by his team mates.' I was thus more than surprised to hear that I had been left out of the side to play against France. 'You did too much on your own. We are aiming for a different style of play on Saturday,' I was told by the management.

So much for Test rugby. To beat the Australians you must match them up front with aggression. The forward play must be tough and with no holds barred. If you give an inch they will walk all over you. We had an idea we would play tick rugby with them. I admit that I was hurt at the selection decision, but a player must take the upsets of rugby, particularly when he is a member of a touring party, and therefore I threw myself into the training at Auckland as eagerly as anyone else.

Rugby League in New Zealand, which is played mainly on an amateur basis, was built round the Union club image with each team working hard to build a club and organizing socials for its finances. The players and officials were really committed to the game in a country obsessed with its Union counterpart. Though the New Zealand authorities looked after our party in a most hospitable manner and spared little expense on our behalf, there was certainly nothing hospitable about Carlaw Park. We failed to adapt ourselves to the foul weather and slippery pitch, while the French, well led by veteran prop-forward Georges Ailléres, produced a monotonous but effective series of high kicks until it finally paid off when Jean Ledru seized on a mistake near our line to score. Capdouze added the goal points, and a penalty by Garrigues later in the game meant they were home, but not dry. We had floundered in the mud in our endeavours to keep the ball moving and many a crucial score had been missed near the line when a player had failed to hold on to the slippery ball. Instead we should have played the French at their own game. A score of 2-7 before this 18,000 crowd was ignominy for the team and we were rightly slated in the press. At the end of the match our players were in tears at the defeat and with the knowledge that we would be denied another crack at the Aussies. The French would now go through to the final match of the World Cup. But I had a point to prove, as did my team mates, in our final game against New Zealand back in Australia at the Sydney Cricket Ground.

We approached this game with a carefree attitude, for little depended on it other than our determination to prove ourselves a sound touring team. The Cricket Ground had a funereal atmosphere with only 14,000 Australians gathered on the terraces, a crowd almost anonymous in such large surroundings. Would Great Britain lose all three games in the World Cup? However, prove ourselves we did as we played the best rugby of the tour to defeat New Zealand 38-14. Free-running from our backs resulted in Clive Sullivan scoring a hat trick of tries, along with others by Ian Brooke, Mick Shoebottom, Arnie Morgan and two from Alan Burwell. Bev Risman kicked seven goals. In the first-half I was revelling in the match and had enjoyed some long runs, being given the breaks by some defence-splitting passes from Charlie Renilson at loose-forward. But tragedy struck. Just before the half-time whistle I was streaking for the line with Tommy Bishop backing up inside, waiting for the scoring pass as we approached the full-back, when a vicious 'short arm tackle' from a covering New Zealander caught me across the chin. My legs wobbled, my senses blurred, and down I fell like a heavyweight at the end of his reign. Three minutes later and with a bottle of smelling salts wasted I was up on my feet but staggering round in such a dazed condition that I was of little use to the side and so was substituted by Cliff Watson. Thus my exit from the World Cup was a sad one after what had initially promised to be a most successful game for me. The Australians became champions by virtue of their defeat of France in the final, while we were left to pick up the pieces of the tour with a string of victories over Queensland at Lang Park, Brisbane, Far North Queensland at

Townsville, and in Mount Isa against a local side.

For a long time Great Britain touring parties have flown thousands of miles to these outposts of Rugby League to provide a special day in the town's calendar once every four years—a day when farmers, miners and cowboys from miles around pour into the stadium for the big match. There is a carnival atmosphere about these games, particularly at Townsville where, in a temperature in the nineties, we easily beat a Far North Queensland side 25-2, but not before the local players had given their all and had a crack at the pommies. Such games were a pleasant relaxation after the World Cup matches—now we were more concerned with sun bathing and swimming than playing rugby. Here was the only time I have ever seen Cliff Watson frightened of anything. Although never afraid of sixteen-stone Aussie forwards, on a midnight swim sheer panic overcame him, followed by a dash for the beach, when our host calmly let drop that, 'We often get sharks along this coast—hope the netting's intact.'

One of the strangest areas in which I have played rugby must surely be Mount Isa, the capital town of North-West Queensland. Here, in Australia's biggest-producing mineral field, set deep in the outback and surrounded by thousands of miles of scrub land, we kicked-off in a temperature of ninety-two degrees at ten o'clock at night. With its cowboys, tough miners and old type wooden saloon bars, it was like playing in Dodge City and certainly Kitty McShane's saloon was no less rough when an after-match reception was held. Only a quick exit by many of the players allowed the timbers to stay up as many a young Aussie, bolstered to overflowing with his lager beer, strutted up and down offering to take on all comers. It is this 'knock me down' attitude which gives Australian rugby its bite. I found it to be the most competitive I had ever played in. Certainly I rued the fact that I went at the latter end of my career for there are fine futures for young aspiring rugby men who are prepared to play them at their own game. We had lost the World Cup, but found a different world of rugby more exciting and satisfying than any I had known.

9
Supporting Characters

For me it was back to the week-by-week slog of League matches, seeming a little dull after the revelations of Australia. I had much to look back on. And by now I was experienced enough to be able to reflect on differences in outlook and character between the codes. In recent seasons the Rugby Union has been indulging in a soul-searching examination of its structure, its coaching and administrative methods, its aims and its needs for players. The game has seen itself become, at times, far too demanding of its top players. Many, such as Mike Burton (Gloucester), Alan Old (Sheffield) and Geoff Evans (Coventry), have opted out of the England squad for various reasons, often through being forced to sit on the substitute's bench for many matches or because of the need to give too much time to international preparations. No longer can the player be a free agent if he wishes to prosper at the highest levels; no longer can he adopt a casual and carefree attitude to his sport as many internationals of the past did. Though I trained as hard, if not harder, than any players today, there was an enormous helping of fun and enjoyment in the Union game and I view with despair the famous names who today leave the clubhouse at the final whistle.

Where is that sense of fun that the St. Helens R.U.F.C. used to take along with it whenever we played away at the Vale of Lune and used to call in at the local pub in Morecambe on the way home? After a furious argument with the landlord, over the question of not being allowed to sing in his lounge bar, I removed his sign—a large Witch's Hat, about four feet high—from the entrance to the pub. Imagine the surprise of an attendant when later in the evening I deposited the metallic hat with a cloakroom attendant for sixpence.

'Will you look after my hat for the evening, madam?'

I never did return, for the local policeman exchanged the ticket for the hat and returned it to an irate but laughing publican.

Such were the escapades which, if somewhat immature, were looked upon with a sense of amazement by the older ex-players who formed the committees and by the voluntary workers who had the task of looking after the players. Men such as Wilf Oldham, or 'Little Wilf' as he was affectionately known in St. Helens, who had been a cripple since birth but whose small stature did not hide his huge heart and biting tongue. If Wilf criticized you, he liked you, and he never praised me once in my life. We always played badly in his eyes. We always did the wrong thing. He loved the club and its players and must have scrubbed well over a thousand baths in his days and pumped up countless balls for us. Ever the master of odd jobs, he was always attended by a scraggy old dog, an emaciated refugee from the R.S.P.C.A.'s mercy squad, named Spotch. Wilf had delusions as to the savagery of this dog and invariably warned passers-by that they were tangling with death if they stood nearby, while the mongrel cowered behind a goal-post. Over twenty years Wilf had three dogs of the same scraggy variety, named Spotch One, Spotch Two and finally Spotch Three.

In that carefree world of Union Rugby, coaching in those days, if it were done at all, was confined to a few words of wisdom from the captain in the bar on a Thursday night. Few players restricted their alcohol intake or curbed their late nights. I can well imagine the reaction of the coach of a present-day Union club if one of his players, as a forward friend of mine at Leeds University once did, stayed up throughout the night to remove the daffodils from the garden in front of his hostel. Pursuing a vendetta with his hostel tutor he snipped the daffodils with scissors and then stuck them in his own garden at home as a present for Mother's Day.

With my conversion to Rugby League, however, I was to meet a more disciplined and dedicated attitude from coaches and committees but with personalities who were no less amusing than their Union counterparts. Of the three coaches during my years with St. Helens R.L.F.C. I saw little of Alan

Prescott, the ex-Great Britain captain, for he left within months of my arrival. But in those early days, he proved to be a warm-hearted and most helpful man to a new Union recruit making his way in the game. Alan, having been the captain at St. Helens in his playing days, seemed to suffer the fate of many player-coaches: he seemed to find it very difficult to exert his discipline and deal with players with whom he had all too recently been a team-mate. I think Alan found it hard to adjust to the change, but it certainly did not dampen his enthusiasm for the game or his professional attitude towards the play. My respect for the demands of the League game and for Alan himself were quickly brought home to me when, during a match against Swinton within a couple of months of signing, I displaced my shoulder in a heavy tackle and suffered what is referred to as a 'sprung shoulder' where the bones overlap. I winced as the trainer helped me from the field and led me, clutching my left shoulder, to the bench.

'I think the shoulder's gone, I fell right on the point.'

'It'll be all right,' he reassured me as we approached the trainer's bench on the half-way line where Alan Prescott, his ginger hair blowing at the sides, sat surveying the scene. With substitutes not allowed in League at that time, he was obviously weighing up the situation.

'Sit here, Ray. Which shoulder? ' he asked, laying his hands on me like some Indian faith-healer, fingers probing beneath my shoulder pads until he struck a large lump of bone on the left. 'Oh it's not so bad this,' and with a quick jerk he man-oeuvred the shoulder back. 'He'll be all right. Ray, tell Dick Huddart you'll pack on the blind side then you only need to push with your right shoulder.'

Who could argue with a man who as captain of the Great Britain team had helped to defeat the Australians in a recent Test match while playing with a broken arm? Within seconds the referee's attention had been caught and I was back in the fray. Both Alan and Stan McCormick, his successor, suffered from the breaking up of the Wembley winning team. For the next three years until 1964 St. Helens was rebuilding, with established players leaving and many Union signings still learning the game. Stan McCormick was thus faced with the daunting task of developing a side which, rather unfortunately for him, he was forced to hand over in 1964.

Stan, a small, dapper, curly-haired wing in his day, was a character of tremendous personality and humour who was the focus of attention wherever he went. In winning the Lancashire Cup and the Western Championship (the competition which replaced the Lancashire League in the single season of 1963/64) he maintained a high team spirit with his quick wit, and was certainly instrumental in helping many of the younger players to develop. His enthusiasm for the game was infectious and, though running a flourishing greengrocer's shop, he was rarely absent from the ground on any day. Nor can it be said that he ever missed a bargain even when we were playing. On one occasion Stan boarded the coach for a match at Hull carrying a battered brown suitcase, offering no explanation as to its contents. The mystery deepened when he asked to be dropped about two miles from the Hull ground and sped away in a taxi. 'He's eloping,' came the cry from Frankie Barrow our full-back in the rear of the coach. Stan, however, remained as secretive as ever even when he arrived for the match minus the suitcase. After a good win and with the team in high spirits, we trooped to the coach not looking forward to the journey home over the Pennines. Suddenly there was uproar from the rear of the bus as huge players leapt off their seats and back into the gangway. Lobsters, which Stan had purchased some hours earlier, had burst out of the suitcase, crawling over the seats and the floor, and were making their way to the driver who clung to his wheel. Stan, seeing his shop's profits about to disappear before his eyes, herded the lobsters to the back seat. There, after restoring them to the case, he settled down for the journey home, with the seat to himself. I could only laugh on my way to school the next morning when, on passing his shop, I caught sight of a blackboard: 'Fresh Lobster. Caught Yesterday.'

Stan's passion for the game was such that his emotions would often get the better of him and it soon became obvious that it was a waste of time for any player to come off the field to have a cut washed or a mouth rinse after three-quarter time, for by then, in his anxiety to win, he had usually drunk the bucket dry. He could also reduce a team to tears as when, on winning the Western Champion- ship against Swinton at Central Park, Wigan, in 1964, I scored the decisive try after a defence-splitting pass from John Tembey in the last seconds. Jubilant, at the final whistle we all turned to mount the steps of the stand for our medals, only to see Stan being carried away from the trainer's dug-out, his face covered in blood. At the moment of my try he had leapt up in the air, forgetting the concrete roof.

I for one was saddened by his final departure and sorry at the manner of his replacement, which reflected the harsh and savage side of professional sport. On our way home from Yorkshire following an evening match, he was abruptly called from the back of the coach, where he had been leading the singing of the players, to the directors' seats at the front. There he was bluntly told he was being asked to resign. It was hardly a lesson in public relations or of choosing the most opportune moment for the Saints. He had worked hard to the best of his ability and deserved better.

Stan was succeeded by Joe Coan, a local schoolmaster who taught physical education. It was a shock appointment, for he had little League pedigree and had no experience of coach- ing a League side. But the appointment by the St. Helens board proved to be a master stroke. Over the next few years the club were to win every available trophy and cup, the highlight being in the 1965/66 season with the winning of the Lancashire Cup, the Lancashire League Cup, the Chall- enge Cup and the Championship Trophy. Joe, while having no expert knowledge of League, brought a high degree of fitness to the sides and a rigid discipline over the players. I have never endured more demanding training-sessions, and usually the whole evening was concentrated on this aspect, for Joe realized that with a team of such talent under him only fitness needed to be his priority. The rugby could look after itself. Tommy Bishop, Alec Murphy, Len Killeen and Tom Van Vollenhoven could score the points, and with eight internationals competing for places in a pack, Joe soared to success. Talented players were at his disposal, most of whom had come to their peak together, and while the situation confirmed one's opinion that 'players make a coach', Joe's efforts, his application and keen attention to discipline, were vital factors in the club's success.

Although I spent only four seasons with Widnes, I again worked with three coaches, two of whom, Joe Egan and Bob Harper, were ex-professional players themselves of the 'old school' type. Both were keen on exercises and fitness training but they suffered from the fact that the team was extremely young and we did not have much experienced talent to give them any basis for success. Though none came keener than Bob, it was Don Gullick, the ex-St. Helens centre of my boyhood, who was to complete my term as a League player. Don, a Welshman and ever controversial, was drunk with rugby. He often spent hours theorizing about the game, holding me enthralled as he pinpointed complicated moves and procedures, occasionally interspersed with the details of the latest biography which he happened to be reading. He must have been the best-read coach in League. He was a firm believer in using the ball, and our evenings were spent playing touch rugby or opposed rugby with Don working tactics into the games. He virtually abandoned the slog of fitness training and preferred to do all the running with the ball much to the annoyance of some of the traditionalists on the Widnes committee. He made sure nobody slacked for he tackled as enthusiastically as anyone. Don enjoyed work with young players, being one of the few coaches in League whom I have seen concentrate on individual skills with a player or small group of players. Far too many in League merely coach the team and assume, because a player is professional, that he has all the necessary skills at his disposal. Concerned for his players, Don always stood up for them, much to the amazement once of a small knot of Widnes supporters who had been barracking the team and Don during one of our poorer displays. Leaping over the wall to confront the spectators, Don gave them the fright of their lives. They did not stand behind the trainer's bench again. Incidentally, it's worth emphasizing that though the players after a poor performance on the field can always escape to the sanctuary of the tunnel, the coach will still have to face up to the directors, wanting their pound of flesh.

Though the towns of St. Helens and Widnes lie only a few miles apart, the approach, attitude and outlook of the two clubs' committees are widely different, or were in my days. To become a member of the Saints' boardroom one has to be invited by the directors, but first the newcomer must hold the requisite number of shares in the club, with the result that it is essentially middle class in outlook and representative of the professions of the town. A mixture in any one year would contain a sprinkling of solicitors, accountants and estate agents complemented by representatives from industry and local business in the shape of haulage contractors, butchers, wholesalers and the like. All these teamed under a chairman, perhaps the most celebrated one in recent years being the long-serving headmaster Harry Cook. Their common binding factor is usually a burning interest in rugby and often a life-long desire to have a stake in the future of what is for many their home-town club. Most of the directors have never played the game and a directorship offers the nearest they can come to fulfilling a desire to be part of the sport. If at times often misguided, particularly in regard to the handling of the players themselves, they spend many hours on the club's behalf receiving little reward save criticism from the public as they go about their business or relax at the golf club. Many, being unable to escape the pressures when bad fortune strikes the team, take the defeats to heart and rarely fail to take it out on player and coach alike, while others, in good times, will watch over the training with a fatherly but patronizing eye as if owners of the livestock parading round the ring.

At St. Helens the relationship between player and director was normally a relaxed one, though as a group the directors tended to be aloof, sitting at the front of the coach and eating at separate tables at dinner. But on reflection this was wise. If directors are to administer a club's finances and see to its welfare, both on and off the field, they must be able to do it without being hindered by any emotional involvement or acquaintance with the players. All had a genuine affection for the League game and watched it with considerable interest, though some watched it closer than others. I remember the time when one particular long-serving and well-respected director visited the dressing-room after one game to praise Bob Dagnall, our hooker, on his scrum figures. Bob was naturally delighted.

'Good game, Bob. You took the scrums four to one in the first-half. What happened in the second-half? You only broke even with him.'

Even Bob Dagnall had not the heart to tell him that he had played second-row in the second-half with Cliff Watson hooking, after a disagreement with the referee.

On another occasion amid a heated discussion in the boardroom on selection, with Stan McCormick presenting his team to the directors, one of them, kindly but forgetful, wanted to know: 'Why are you preferring Keith Northey on the wing to Len Killeen? '

'Because Killeen is on his holidays in South Africa and has been there for three weeks,' came the reply.

The winning of countless trophies over the past twenty-five years is sure testimony to the directors' methods at St. Helens as opposed to the much more open and informal relationships which, possibly due to the profusion of ex-players on the committee, existed in my time at Widnes. When the Saints' directors went away on a match they went as if on a trip 'to do business', but the Widnes committee went away for 'a night out'.

As captain at Widnes, I was regularly listened to in friendly discussions on the way from a match and often my advice would be taken, whereas during my spell as captain at St. Helens the position only operated on the field and little notice was taken of it. At Widnes, following a good win away from home, we would often be led in singing by the committee, following the strains of Jack Hayes, the ex-Widnes hooker and committee man. At St. Helens, the directors read their evening newspapers. There was a more relaxed club atmosphere at Widnes with everyone straining earnestly for the success of the side, the committee working alongside the supporters' club members in a common cause. I particularly enjoyed my career there for I could not have been better treated, but again on reflection, the fact that in four seasons from 1967 to 1971 we won few trophies indicates perhaps a too casual attitude towards the players.

One committee man who could certainly relax the players was 'Batty' Foran, a well-known bookmaker in the town, who always came up smiling no matter what the result. Batty, happy-go-lucky, would endear himself to the players by increasing our winning bonus after a good performance and often he would slip into the dressing-room at half-time and add a few pounds to the bonus if we were playing well. The adrenalin often flowed faster in the second-half as a result. However, the only time I saw Batty worried was after one of his half-time visits to our dressing-room in a match at Leeds during the first round of a championship play-off. I was naturally delighted at the way the game had gone for us as we led Leeds at the half-time whistle and I was hurriedly patting all my players on the back on our way to the dressing-room for a breather. Leeds had been strong favourites not only to beat Widnes in this first round but also to take the championship and as I urged each one to 'keep it up in the second-half' there was delight on their faces. Many of the committee had come down from the directors' box in the stand to add their congratulations and offer advice as to how the second-half might be played. Batty's head popped around the door.

'Marvellous performance, lads. Ray, you're on £50 per man if you can win it.'

Silence. All ears strained waiting for Batty to continue.

'Get them beat and I'll add it to your pay packets.' 'Extra £50 per man. Hell, I'd tackle my grandmother for that', were the thoughts flooding through everyone's heads.

Not quite sure what Batty had meant—an extra £50 would have put us on £100 for a first-round win—I was urged to ask, 'Batty, do you mean £50 *per man*?' realizing he had meant the sum to be divided.

Batty, flushed with enthusiasm, but realizing he had made a mistake, still stuck by his offer and proved a man of his word.

'Come on, lads, let's get this one won. Knock 'em down, there's £100 here,' I implored as we trooped through the crowd and on to the field for the beginning of the second-half.

Batty had returned to the stand with assistance and weak at the knees, having calculated that thirteen players plus two substitutes at £50 per head equalled £750. For thirty-five minutes we tackled like demons as Batty sat gripped to his seat watching the battle to keep our lead, but unfortunately, or fortunately, Leeds snatched glory in the dying seconds and took £100 from our grasp. The colour returned to Batty's cheeks, but such was his enthusiasm and passion for the club and its players nobody doubted that had we won we would all have benefited. Whether in relief, or appreciation, he still added a fiver to our losing pay, typifying the spirit within the club.

Thanks to the guidance of such coaches and committee men at St. Helens and Widnes, I was able to reach the heights in Rugby League. For many players, however, the world of League is far removed from the medals, cups and trophies which adorn the sideboards of the major clubs. At clubs like Huyton, Batley and Doncaster their season is a hard grind as year after year they fight for their existence, coping financially on less gates than a middle-sized Union club. The committee men here are the really dedicated workers, devising fund-raising schemes to supplement the attendances which can often figure in hundreds rather than the hoped-for thousands. Their optimism springs eternal for that one lucky break. For the players with a lowly club the League game represents a way of life, an enjoyment, a couple of nights training and a game at weekends. It is an outlet from work. Only the hope of being spotted by a major club can spur them on, for, often as not earning only losing pay, they can take home little more than a barman in a pub. But the spirit and enthusiasm of these clubs never fails to surprise me.

Perhaps nowhere is the true grit and community spirit seen in greater abundance than in the twin Cumbrian outposts of Whitehaven and Workington, two towns perched on the coast at the extremities of League country. The hardness and down-to-earth approach of their players often matches the bleak approaches to their grounds. Both teams have had their great days, particularly Workington in the Gus Risman era and in the fifties. We players at Widnes and St. Helens never relished the long trip up there for I can never remember playing other than in gale-force winds and driving rain. Either because of the harsh weather or the rugged farming country around, we were always met by some of the toughest and strongest forwards in the game. Their record in producing men such as Dick Huddart, John Tembey, Brian Edgar and Bill Martin is second to none. They certainly produced partisan spectators too, who, locked in this isolated outpost, raised their side to great heights and upset many visitors. At Whitehaven, for example, one celebrated old lady of Herculean proportions used to stand on a mound near the pathway through the crowd to the visitors' dressing-room and happily beat any player over the head with her umbrella if he had displeased her.

Matches at Workington were hard-fought, with forward play dominating the proceedings, but coupled to the strong running of Ike Southward and Harry Archer, two Cumbrians born and bred. The games, however, were not without their lighter moments, as in the saga which ran for two matches between myself and Alec Murphy and Workington's Dennis Martin and Brian Edgar. The incidents had their beginnings in a Saints v Workington match at St. Helens when Alec, Bill Martin and myself were all sent off the field despite my having had little to do with the original incident. As Bill Martin was tackled near the touch-line Alec calmly strolled along and kicked him up the backside and then scooted away, while I, waiting nearby to mark him at the 'play the ball', stood laughing. Bill, enraged and thinking it was me, planted a lovely punch on my chin and as we locked together along came the referee to dismiss all three of us. Although we laughed about the incident afterwards, it was not forgotten when we arrived at Workington later in the season. Alec, cheeky as ever, started his tricks by having another go at their two forwards, telling them from a distance: 'Frenchie'll do you, Bill. Do him, Ray.'

Frenchie did not feel like 'doing' anybody, least of all the Workington pack before their own fanatical band of supporters, and as things became over-heated I was called out by the referee Peter Geraghty immediately in front of the most vociferous section.

'Get him off, ref, the dirty so and so...'

94

Peter, an understanding referee and a man always on pleasant terms with the players, wagged his finger at me and said, 'Ray, I'm wagging my finger at you and shouting for their benefit. It's been a good game, don't spoil it. How's your wife keeping, all right? Family okay? Are you still teaching? '

'Let him have it, ref, you tell him.'

'That's long enough now, Ray, they're happy.'

Peter understood his players.

Though such long trips in mid-winter are often looked upon with dismay by many players, the journeys, with their endless card games, do contribute to the spirit of the team. The trip home would be broken for a few hours at an inn or hotel for dinner and drinks. Many Union players are often dissuaded from signing for League by statements that their social life will suffer, but I have found this to be the complete opposite and on many a trip home we have enjoyed ourselves; once, however, on false hopes.

'Everton v Leeds United... Draw. Carlisle v Blackburn Rovers... Draw.' I called out our list of draws on the Vernons Treble Chance for that week to Basil Lowe, the secretary, who was carefully scrutinizing the stop-press column of the early edition Saturday evening paper. We were at the Three Nuns Hotel near Huddersfield on the way back from a good away victory and before dinner I had suggested that we check our weekly perm on the pools which I ran on behalf of twenty-seven players at a shilling a week.

'We've won, we have eight draws.'

'Ridiculous, impossible. Here let me check,' insisted Len Killeen. 'He's right, we have. But all the results are not here; still that doesn't affect ours, does it?'

'What's £250,000 divided by twenty-seven? It's about £9,000 each. I think I'll retire,' observed Cliff Watson.

'Better check with the full paper when we get back to St. Helens, you get some misprints in the stop press,' remarked Basil Lowe again.

Few cared as we celebrated with drinks and sang all the way home in the coach until all huddled round the newspaper seller at the St. Helens Town Hall.

'Eh, we do have eight draws, lads, but there's twenty-three on this week.'

'It'll not be £250,000.'

It certainly was not. Six days later I received a credit note for two shillings and sixpence to be divided by twenty-seven.

Of all the personalities I encountered in the League game, few were more interesting than the bunch of Fijians who signed for Rochdale Hornets in the mid-sixties and provided considerable interest for the spectators during their short stay. Happy and carefree characters, they looked a strange sight as they journeyed from ground to ground in their huge, army greatcoats supplied by the Rochdale club. They were the only coats big enough and warm enough for the Fijians' enormous frames. They figured as the gentle giants of the sport with massive shoulders and strapping thighs ideally suited for a physical contest. Strong and fast, their large feet covered acres of ground and it was reputed that the Rochdale scrum-half could stand in their boots with his own boots on. Levula, Ravouvou, Toga, Drui—their exotic names filled many a programme in our Northern towns. More than one player will recall their bone-crunching runs at their opponents, none more so than my ex-St. Helens colleagues Peter Harvey and Keith Northey, who were both felled by the sheer strength of Joe Levula on the wing. I well remember Peter, prostrate on the floor, recovering his senses and feeling every bruise in his five foot six inches, looking up at a smiling face and the enquiring eyes of a six-foot giant who casually remarked, 'Sorry. Hope you're not hurt,' and he meant it. Peter groaned in disbelief.

10
Time Called

My League career began after anxious months of pondering and analysing. But its end was abrupt, the outcome of a sudden impulse in the early hours of a dismal morning. Many travellers who have been forced to cross the Pennines at dead of night have sought refuge in a transport café for the delights of bacon butties and a large mug of tea. Widnes were no exception as we trooped into 'Ted's' on a wind-swept, rain-lashed Pennine road at two o'clock on a Saturday morning, after an exhausting trip to Humberside. It was the last week of the 1971 season and there was little at stake save the completion of fixtures. The match at Hull on that Friday evening was a particularly difficult one. Players had to leave work early and there was also the not too pleasant prospect of a long coach trip. It had been an eventful, amusing, but tiring day for us all, as we sat slumped over the formica tables, warming our hands round the hot mugs.

For myself it was to be the end not only of a long day which had begun at eight o'clock that morning, but of a long career. I had met the coach outside the school gates at three o'clock, having taught six lessons to an assort-ment of eleven- to eighteen-year-olds and, carrying a pile of exercise books to be marked on the journey, I was greeted with the news that three of the regular players were not playing—'bad stomach', 'sore shins', 'can't get off work'. This was the usual tale of woe for such a trip at the end of a season. Few believed the excuses but one could hardly blame a player who had to weigh up the probability of losing £10 for the loss of a shift against the possibility of £6 for a defeat at Hull. Still, there were many young lads willing to have a go. Widnes were never short in that department but in the club's happy-go-lucky atmosphere we were short of a tea a couple of hours later, when it was realized that none of the committee present knew the name of the hotel in Wakefield into which we had been booked. Hence the curious sight of the Widnes team coach criss-crossing the centre of Wakefield, stopping at every hotel to ask, 'Have Widnes booked in here for tea? ' This aroused considerable delight until, finding the correct hotel awkwardly situated on a roundabout, we quickly filed in, picked up our steaks in serviettes and rejoined the coach on its way back round the roundabout. The search for the steaks meant a delay in the kick-off and forced us to change in the coach as we journeyed through Hull town-centre, but it did not dampen our enthusiasm for we were only beaten by a couple of points in a high-scoring match. Despite all the frustrations, I had enjoyed myself and had been in the thick of the game to such an extent that Don Gullick, the coach, joked that I was 'running like a two-year old'. This praise, however, could not hide my lack of enthusiasm for the game. Now thirty-two years old, my appetite had gone and I was much more concerned by the performances of my school teams than my own, a state of affairs which I found difficult to hide from the club and from Don. Two o'clock in the morning in a transport café may hardly be the most appropriate time to retire, but I felt I could no longer do justice to myself and I felt I should not let the club down. Don, who was staggered at the sudden decision, must have known the moment in his own career for his only words were, 'You're right, Ray. Never grow old in this game.'

I was possibly open to criticism in retiring with only four games left in the season, although if I had continued I would not have been fair to a club who had always done their best for me, and I believed that those last four games would give Don time to experiment for the following year. It came as a relief to have the weight taken from my shoulders. There was no sorrow at my departure, nothing like the sadness I had felt at my transfer. I was ready for retirement. The game had become a chore and was no longer a source of enjoyment. I yearned for another interest and was to find it in coaching, but not Rugby League. Surprisingly, it was Rugby Union that now claimed my attentions again.

Despite ten seasons of the League game, during which time I managed to mould my face with a cauliflower ear, flattened nose and scarred eyebrows in almost four hundred games, I was determined never to lose contact with the Union game and for this my teaching profession has suited me admirably. In my early years at St. Helens I introduced Union to Fairfield School, Widnes, and, on Saturday mornings prior to Saints' matches, I could frequently be seen refereeing a match or serving 'pie and mash' in the school canteen afterwards. If a boy was injured on the field, a trip to the hospital at Whiston would often be followed by a dash to the Saints' ground for the afternoon kick-off with my mind hardly centred on a big League clash; but it was all worth it. It was enjoyable and rewarding and I was more than grateful to be allowed to continue with the schoolboy rugby on my return to my old school at Cowley, St. Helens. With League being played more and more on Friday evenings and Sunday afternoons to avoid the television clash, I soon settled into a routine which was to straddle both codes. Now I looked forward to many hours of enjoyment on the school fields coaching Cowley rugby free from the pressures and controversy of club football. Little did I know what Wally Ashcroft, brother of my old friend Alan Ashcroft, the British Lion, had in store for me.

Wally urged me to help in coaching at St. Helens R.U.F.C. who had just experienced the worst season in the club's history and, in losing players to League and major Union clubs, had few prospects. The offer was appealing. The shrewd officers of the club could see the opportunities for the club, while I could see the advantage for my school and its players. The club was to get its hands on one of the finest nurseries of rugby talent in the country—a school which had produced more county players than any other school, six full internationals and in the last ten years more international schoolboys than any other establishment. They would have a basis for success. I welcomed the opportunity to coach at club level, to try out new ideas and, above all, to maintain my relationship in rugby with my boys after they left school. Over seventy-five per cent of all schools' 1st XV players have finished with the game inside five years of leaving; I hoped to encourage ours to continue and develop in their home town. My school teams could use the senior club's facilities and floodlights; the club could use the school's expertise in coaching and administration. Under my fanciful title of 'schools' liaison officer', therefore, I soon set to work. Seeing the need for ruthless methods, I had scrapped a full St. Helens team within three months of my arrival and was prepared to take defeat after defeat as I went back to basics and discipline with a team of eighteen- and nineteen-year-olds. They were happy if hectic days, as, eager to learn and work, they trained late into the night and, I hope, gained much more from it. Certainly their attitude changed. Gone was the old 'kick around or tick rugby tonight, lads? ' routine. They wanted to succeed and within three years we broke more than even on results and were well on the way to maturity. The club spirit was being rekindled, pride in achievement was returning, and in possessing at least fifteen Lancashire schoolboys and five England schools' internationals, coupled with the local schools' League talent, I must have had the best squad around.

However, all was not a bed of roses, for off the field, as an ex-Rugby League player, I had to maintain a low profile in the clubhouses and with visiting teams pose as the schools' liaison officer or maintain that I had just come to watch a few of my ex-schoolboys. We had to meet many hours before the kick-off in a Sunday cup match so that I could give a team talk without fear of provoking the opposite side. At many an important game, I have strolled up casually with a couple of friends deliberately ten minutes late so as not to arouse suspicion. Contrary to expectations few bothered and at most clubs my coaching became common knowledge, to such an extent that I was welcomed most warmly by many first-class clubs in my coaching capacity. Endless discussions ensued after matches with visiting committees on such things as tactics and training methods, without rancour, for there is little antagonism between the games in the North—indeed while I was coaching at St. Helens, others like Derek Hurt (ex-Leigh R.L.) and Don Gullick (ex-St. Helens R.L.) were all assisting Union clubs in Lancashire and Cheshire. But I could never be sure of my reception and went to great lengths to disguise my role, often with hilarious results.

For one game with a first-class Yorkshire club it was decided I should travel by car and arrive late at the ground, only calling by chance to see eight of my ex-Cowley schoolboys play. I did arrive late and stood quietly alone at the side of the grandstand, hoping to be inconspicuous during the play while afterwards in the clubhouse I chatted in a corner to a couple of the players.

'Ray. How are you? Nice to see you.'

I cringed as I was greeted by one of the club's committee men and immediately had my cover story all lined up. He had only to trigger the words and your happy, friendly schools' liaison officer would be in full flow.

'Fine young side you have there, coming along nicely,' he smiled.

What could I say? I felt others round me on edge and listening. 'Oh yes, they have improved considerably since I had them at school. I thought I would pop over to see them while I had a free Saturday,' I replied.

'Come off it, you rogue. Here, come here,' and he proceeded to propel me to a large figure who was standing with his back to us, discussing the game with a small group of players. 'Meet our coach, Ray, he knows you.'

The large back turned. He certainly did know me. It was Dave Valentine, the ex-Huddersfield, Yorkshire and Great Britain captain.

Other times were not so humorous, and often I was saddened and shamed at being forced to keep well away from a changing-room before kick-off, unable to speak to young men whom I had first known as tiny eleven-year-olds on my school fields and in my classrooms, eleven-year-olds whom I had helped and was proud of. Secretly and furtively I would pass messages to them during a match as I stood outside in the rain or sleet of a wintry afternoon. I have indeed felt despised and been made to feel unwanted by many who have little to contribute to Union other than the bar profits. It is a funny feeling inside to see my work displayed and admired and myself despised for being successful. Nevertheless we continued until, after one warning from the Lancashire Rugby Union committee, it was necessary to try to strengthen the illusion of the schools' liaison officer. On one rain-swept night, therefore, when the full Lancashire team were in training at the St. Helens R.U. ground at Moss Lane prior to a county game, I deliberately coached my school team on the next pitch and vainly tried to give the impression to any county committee members present that I was merely using St. Helens Rugby Union Club's facilities to coach my school side. By chatting to old acquaintances in the bar afterwards, we hoped to convince any officials present that all was well at St. Helens and that the club really was simply allowing its grounds to be used by local schools. Sadly, our trick failed, for within three months a further curt letter asking for clarification arrived on our secretary's desk. Many were for seeing the matter through and challenging the system. Others, whom I feel were unable to keep pace with the progress which the club was making, wished to settle for a quiet life. I desired none of it and retired sadly from my post.

I still find it hard to believe that after eight years of nursing and caring for a boy during his career at school, when he passes through the school gates I am unable to offer him help and advice in his chosen sport, advice which might help the sport as well. As a teacher, over the last fifteen years I have coached, organized matches and arranged tours for boys up to the age of eighteen. But to be asked to stop dealing with them once they have reached this mystical age, I find inexplicable. St. Helens R.U.F.C. was the loser, for within weeks of my departure at least a dozen players, by now accustomed to regular coaching and demanding dedication to the game, had left for major clubs and were to gain honours in the game. Within twelve months Waterloo were John Player Cup finalists after signing my ex-school players Ian Ball (now with Barrow R.L.F.C.), Dave Carfoot (both Lancashire and England Under-23s), Steve Tickle (then their captain, now also with Barrow R.L.F.C.) and many others. Orrell wecomed John Ireland (Lancashire hooker) to add to another ex-pupil Dave Gullick (Lancashire and England trials), while Mike Guest went on to captain Widnes to the Lancashire Cup in 1976. They and many others deserved their honour and rewards for they had earned it as teenagers in our battle to remedy an ailing club. We had been within an ace of succeeding but in the words of Alan Gott, the Lancashire secretary: 'There are laws in the Rugby Union code and we as a constituent body have to abide by those laws.'

Of course any member of an organization should abide by that organization's laws but the game surely is riddled with hypocrisy when, within twelve months of departure, I had been approached by five major clubs in the Northern merit table with a view to coaching their 1st XVs—the very clubs which had sat in judgement on St. Helens. Surely my term at St. Helens had helped to better the club, improve the players, and in encouraging players of the calibre of Dave Carfoot, Ian Ball, Dave Gullick and John Horton, I had not neglected the county either.

To many outside the four League counties, the occasional sensational newspaper headline describing the banning of a League player from a team or from a clubhouse would seem to indicate an atmosphere of open hostility between the two codes with players and committees steering well clear of each other. Nothing could be further from the truth, for in the North there is usually harmony between the codes, friendships among players and committees and respect for each other's game. The 'old school tie' Union member will find it difficult to understand how the St. Helens Round Table could organize a Rugby League Sevens tournament with all profits going to the benefit of the town's League-playing schools, plus a cheque of £175 for Cowley School's Union trip to South America. They would be surprised at the countless numbers of Union internationals, county players, and schoolboys who have sat on Frank Tobin's physiotherapist's bench at Widnes Rugby League club where, without payment, he has worked many hours to get them fit for their next Union match. They would not be amused at a Lancashire Schools' meeting held a few years ago in St. Helens when all the schoolmasters present were ex-League players. All therefore were ineligible to act as selectors in the county trials, with the result that the trial had to be postponed, despite their keen interest in schoolboy rugby —a law now thankfully amended.

The Rugby Union maintains that the strength of its case

is centred round the desire to retain an amateur game, and that it is a most praiseworthy aim in sport's sad decline into the world of commercialism and cheap gimmickry. But surely this anti-professionalism is merely a smokescreen. Take, for example, the welcome given to full-time professional sportsmen such as Frank Hayes, the Lancashire and England cricketer, at Broughton Park R.U. club, and to Bob Gaskell, the ex-Manchester United goalkeeper, at Wrexham R.U. club—players who have earned more in a month's play than a League player in a season. Here is no anti-professionalism.

There was also the ludicrous situation when a young man of twenty was refused permission to play for his Union team because he had played for a local amateur League side in Barrow above the age of eighteen. The fact that he was a convicted murderer and hoping to play for his prison side did not enter into the banning! The decline in the respect for referees and discipline at soccer games, and the attendant violence which is now turning schools away from the game, places rugby in a premier position as a winter sport. League thrives at the grassroots and Union is at the peak of its popularity, yet both codes, by being apart, are currently grappling with problems which must be solved in the near future.

The influx of leagues, cups and increased competition in the Union game has certainly created problems for the demands on clubs and players are now similar to their professional counterparts. While all clubs strive to win national trophies and their area merit tables, the extra travelling and pre-match preparations are straining the purse strings. Full-time stewards and groundsmen, and nation-wide fixtures, all demand greater money-raising ventures than the odd raffle or players' dance. Many of the clubs must become 'gate-taking' clubs and, as in the case of Orrell, a club which has notably strengthened its fixture list, undertake long and costly journeys to Wales, Scotland and London. Indeed, three Northern clubs, Huddersfield, Hartlepool Rovers and Middlesbrough, threatened legal action against the R.F.U. after they had been omitted from the Northern merit table in the season 1977/78, an omission which they believed would cause them considerable loss of revenue.

The demands on today's top players are far removed from the original concept of amateurism. An ordinary working man, faced with club training, county training and England squad sessions, may have to decide whether he wants to rise in the game at the expense of his job. It is significant how many players have opted out of international rugby in recent seasons. The British Lions' tour to New Zealand in 1977 highlighted the problems a long overseas tour can bring. Many internationals were unable to make the trip because of their work commitments or for fear of losing their jobs. Others, like schoolmasters, who receive no pay while away from home, have to make tremendous sacrifices to pay for such trips. Dr. Danie Craven, the South African rugby president, and ever a true amateur, recently concluded that he could not see why '...one player on tour should suffer loss of wages while another enjoys full pay. The difference should be met by the Unions concerned. Rugby is growing at a tremendous rate throughout the world so we cannot continue with an approach which was acceptable during the last century.'

The solution for the Union game is not an easy one, for it has reached the situation faced by the early pioneers of Rugby League in the 1900s—an increased demand for competition and leagues from the players but greater demands on the finances of the clubs who move nearer to their professional brethren in attitude. They face the problem of the old 'broken-time payments' which first caused the split; players need expenses to play at the highest levels. As Union reluctantly moves nearer to the professional code so its troubles and stresses hit at its amateur basis. Conversely, as League, the professional code, struggles more and more with its finances so it is forced to encourage the development of amateur Rugby League with its reservoir of potential recruits.

The League game has to some extent gone backwards in the last twenty years, and its crowds are sparse compared with those before the mid-fifties. Despite a rapid increase in gates in the last two or three years, we have now reached a situation where virtually no club can exist on its gate receipts

105

and many have been forced to adopt the Australian practice of adding social facilities in the shape of restaurants, discos and bars, further to increase revenue. Some, as at Salford, have been successful, but others in smaller towns faced with stiff competition from local night clubs and Labour clubs have fared badly. St. Helens lost £19,000 on their social complex in the season 1976/77.

Clubs' match payments have been unable to keep pace with inflation and an average winning wage of £45 today compares badly with a wage of £20 in 1960. The low 'A' team wages and only moderate signing fees for Union stars have meant that many youngsters who are highly paid in their normal employment are not attracted to the game for such a low return. Faced with the prospect of earning about £8 less tax, many 'A' teams fail to attract the right player and are forced to include the eternal trialist under the names of A.N. Other and A. Newman. The saturation coverage of the game on television, where 'our Eddie' entertains millions every week with his commentaries, has undoubtedly taken many from the terraces, perhaps never to return. Thus League is more than ever dependent on the annual television fee. Unlike many people, I think that Eddie Waring has done much for the game, giving it a national standing which it never previously had. Without him and television, we would not have such companies as Esso, Forward Chemicals, Forshaws Breweries, Trumans and Mackeson sponsoring games.

Faced with these new aspects of professionalism, the League game has turned back to its amateur roots, an aspect of the code which has been disastrously neglected in the past by the senior clubs and in particular at Chapeltown Road, Leeds, the Rugby League's headquarters. The strides taken by the British Amateur Rugby League Association (B.A.R.L.A.) have been staggering and their work over the last few years deserves the highest praise and respect. With the opening of their fine new head-quarters in Huddersfield by Dennis Howell, Minister for Sport, in September 1977, they were set for even further expansion. The newspapers of my own area are littered with the names of amateur pub, club and works teams all involved in local leagues. In the area comprising St. Helens, Wigan, Warrington and Widnes there are now three divisions of 'open age' amateur teams, forty-nine in all, allied to Under-18 and Under-16 leagues as well. A recent tour of Australia for Under-18s was followed by an 'open age' trip to Papua and New Guinea. Clubs such as Widnes Tigers, coached by international referee Mick Naughton, thrive with Under-15-, 14-, 13-, 12- and 11-year-old sides for schoolboys on a Sunday. Professional players are giving regular coaching sessions, and such is the new-found enthusiasm that for the first time Rugby Union sides are experiencing difficulty in maintaining colts' teams as youngsters move to the League game, while the odd Union club such as Heinz in Wigan has even changed over to the League code. Amateur teams abound as far apart as London, Portsmouth, Oxford and Glasgow and the story of their growth is an unqualified success. The recently formed Universities, Polytechnics and Colleges leagues, backed by N.U.S. funds, coupled with the introduction of Rugby League coaching as part of the curriculum in physical education colleges, seems to guarantee the future of the code.

The Rugby Union, by shutting its door firmly against the amateur player of the other code, now supported by no less a body than the Sports Council, is making a huge mistake for it could be destructive to itself and harmful to its image as a sport to be enjoyed to the full by the true amateur. The insistence of the Rugby Union in refusing to allow an amateur player the right to transfer from League to Union is damaging to its reputation and is out of place in our society. Their governing body refuse to do so because, they claim, an amateur team may play against a professional team in the Rugby League Challenge Cup and would thereby forfeit its amateur status. Why should Rugby Union cling so obstinately to senseless and outdated rules which inhibit the game's development for the enjoyment of all?

11
Different Codes, Different Styles

This is the time when League and Union should be moving closer together, trying to understand and cooperate with each other instead of fighting a cold war. There is no need for an iron curtain between two sets of sportsmen who share most of the same ideals. Despite the difficulties and differences which occur off the field, on the field the last ten years has seen the two games come much closer together from a playing point of view. Though many similar positions in a team still carry out vastly different functions in each code, the pattern of play in Union has been brought closer to that of the modern League by adapting many of its laws, particularly those which give the game its reputation for open play. The proud boast of Union has always been that it was a players' game, and though many crowds and television viewers of the late fifties and early sixties bemoaned the continual kicking to touch in international matches, few administrators gave them much sympathy. Most spectators at the local Union ground were players, ex-players, or friends of the members, but the situation has now changed dramatically and the increase in popularity of the game as a spectacle has been attended by a corresponding upsurge in spectator interest.

The Union laws which have been borrowed from League have all contributed to the opening up of play and the increase in running of the backs. The revision of the law relating to the 'knock on', with the ball now having to be knocked to the ground, caused less stoppages in the three-quarter-movements, while the difference in points between a try and a penalty goal (four points to three points) brought the game in line with the League differential of three points to two points. The latter alteration certainly placed the emphasis on the scoring of tries at the expense of the penalty goal. Gone are the days when a simple penalty infringement would be the equal of a sixty- or seventy-yard try. The differential penalty has again rid the game of its old over-emphasis on the penalty goal, and it is a pleasure to see thought given to the many variations on the tap penalty, all resulting in a greater inclination to run with the ball. Perhaps the most far-reaching legislation was the introduction of the law making it necessary for the ball to bounce before finding touch when a player is kicking outside his twenty-two-metre line, the direct kick to touch only being retained inside this area. The effect upon play has been startling and, though not adopting the full League law here, has meant a far greater emphasis on running from the inside backs, or linking with the forwards, rather than the traditional cry of 'when in doubt boot the ball out.'

When players of the calibre of Lewis Jones, Billy Boston and others left the valleys of Wales to sign professional forms, they knew that they were also going to gain far greater opportunities to display their talents. Today, Gareth Edwards, Gerald Davies and Phil Bennett have had no need to move from Union to display their attacking potential; the opportunities are now abundant in the game as clearly demonstrated by Phil Bennett. Try-scoring and high scores are now commonplace—even in international matches. Union has taken the best from League and has retained its basic strength, that of the wide gulf between forwards and backs. Though the ruck and the mauls might seem an untidy mess to the casual spectator, with the line-outs all shoving and barging, they nevertheless have the function of bringing forwards together, taking them out of the game and allowing space for the backs to run. The forwards have never lost their primary role of ball-getters in Union and therefore big men are still necessary for this task. In League, the whole emphasis of forward play has changed through the alteration of the laws in the mid-sixties, with devastating effects upon the game.

Few realize that in 1961 the League's administrators experimented with the idea of releasing the ball in the tackle, as the Union player is forced to do. Some gave serious thought to its adoption long before the introduction of the 'four-tackle rule' (now amended to six) in season 1966/67, whereby a League team has only that set number of tackles to absorb before the referee calls a scrummage. Such thinking rapidly evaporated when administrators witnessed the unique experimental match arranged between a British team and a French side at the Parc des Princes, Paris, in the October of 1961. The fixture was also one of the League's first ventures into sponsorship, with the participation of the French car firm Renault. The game was played under League rules but the ball had to be released when the player carrying it was stopped. As the programme notes indicated, 'After a tackle, when the ball touches the ground, it is playable by the foot or the hand of all the other players in both teams.' In order to give such a ruling the best possible chance to succeed, the players selected were those who had had considerable experience in Union. And the French side included the redoutable Lacaze at full-back, Mantoulan at stand-off and Savonne on the wing. The English side contained a galaxy of ex-international Union players and should have been ideally suited to take advantage of the experiment. With Bev Risman (ex-England) and Shillinglaw (ex-Scotland) combining as half-backs and ex-South African players Griffiths, Tom Van Vollenhoven, Skene, Greenwood and Jan Prinsloo completing the back division, there was no lack of skill. Up front, ex-Wales Danny Harris and myself made a second-row partnership while Sos Sayer (St. Helens and Great Britain) hooked, for then, as now, ex-Union hookers were at a premium.

Despite all the preparation and careful thought given to the selection of the teams, the game was a disaster and many of us spent the whole evening scratching and scrambling on the floor for the ball. There was little opportunity to develop what might be termed a maul or ruck as in Union. With a couple of forwards on the floor the two or three remaining were not sufficient to develop anything constructive and the game soon developed into basketball with the ball-carrier trying to avoid a tackle at all costs. Forwards had developed new techniques and could not apply themselves to their old styles. The ball was propelled sideways, backwards, even forwards, at a frantic pace until by half-time the thirteen men on either side, vainly trying to play a combination of both codes, could hardly walk from the field through fatigue.

The second-half was played at virtually walking pace with no physical contact, for any British League player took his life into his hands when diving to the ground for the ball. The French boots seemed to be everywhere. The game had few stoppages and players were unable to keep up with the pace for there were no pauses for infringements at line-outs, rucks or mauls as are normal in Union. Sos Sayer summed it up much later in the evening when, munching a bag of chestnuts and attempting to cut a fashionable figure in a pavement café on the Champs Elysées, he was heard to remark, 'If this rule comes in I'll have to retire or get a new pair of bloody legs.' Yet despite this disaster, that colourful French weekend was the beginning of plans to scrap the accepted system of 'unlimited possession'.

Those who changed this facet of the game have invariably argued that the game was being stifled by sides who were 'stuffing the ball up their jerseys'. The advocates of the limited tackle law would have us believe that there were countless games where teams plodded downfield merely holding on to the ball to rob opponents of any chance of victory in the last ten minutes. Granted there may have been some, but I firmly believe that this single change has completely reshaped a team's approach for the worse. Possession of the ball for lengthy periods enabled sides to develop world-class players who could command the use of the ball to show their tricks. Sides could probe and set up an endless variety of moves, particularly among the forwards. It was an era of great ball-playing forwards such as Vince Karalius (St. Helens and Widnes), Johnny Whiteley (Hull), Rocky Turner (Wakefield Trinity) and the legendary Brian McTigue (Wigan)—all big men who brought forward skills to a fine art, providing the defence-splitting passes and subtle sleight-of-hand for men of the calibre of Dick Huddart (St. Helens), Roy Evans (Wigan) and Don Vines (Wakefield Trinity) to run to. Forward play was kept to the middle of the field. The tackling of these fifteen- and sixteen-stone giants was bone crushing and their direct running energy sapping. The result was that forwards rarely appeared in a back line as they do today. As teams attacked their opponents' line the crowd stood with bated breath. 'Could the defence hold out?' 'Would the attacking side get over the line?' Both sets of fans urged on their favourites until they were hoarse. The 'oohs' and the 'aahs' could be heard all round the town. Nowadays the fans merely count the tackles until the six are used up and even though a team is only one yard from the line, the game is stopped in an artificial manner. A scrum ensues, and the rising tension within the crowd has been deflated at one blow of the whistle.

A traditionalist like myself is frequently attacked by comments to the effect that the game is much faster and more fluent today, that the tedious forward battles are 'a thing of the past'. But how justified are these arguments when the top try-scorer in League will barely reach thirty tries a season today? Did not Dick Huddart average thirty tries a season when he was playing second-row? Where are today's equivalents of Tom Van Vollenhoven (St. Helens), Brian Bevan (Warrington), Billy Boston (Wigan), Lionel Cooper (Huddersfield) and Brian Nordgren (Wigan), who averaged sixty to seventy tries a season on the wings? Not one wingman but half a dozen players regularly reached these figures. If a club's complete threequarter-line scores sixty tries in a season they are to be complimented under the present laws. The 'stuffing the ball up the jersey' routine must have been short lived when teams such as St. Helens, Wigan and Huddersfield were topping 1,000 points a season. The game produced star players in outstanding sides who had ample opportunity to display their talents on the weaker brethren and usually before the lesser club's largest crowd of the season. People flocked to see spectacular tries. One spectator summed it up admirably at a recent match I attended when he remarked, 'Communism in rugby—all players are equal.' The solid grafter is now at a premium. Teams have been evened up and the standards have been levelled down, not up. The minnows of the game can keep in contact with the giants for far too long in a match. While Halifax's recent record defeat by a Hull amateur side is testimony to the fine work over the years by the B.A.R.L.A. it is a condemnation of our professional standards. What value can be gained from a £15,000 signing if he can only handle the ball in a relatively short period of play before the six-tackle rule necessitates a scrum? The world of League was almost given the shock of its life in two successive seasons in 1977 and 1978 by the St. Helens amateur side Pilkington Recs who narrowly failed to progress to the second round of the Challenge Cup at the expense of the mighty Wigan and Castleford, two teams with proud cup-fighting traditions. Pilkington Recs, ably coached by ex-Great Britain star Austin Rhodes, have a long and illustrious history both as a professional club before the Second World War and more recently as one of the forerunners of the amateur movement. Supported by the Pilkington Glass firm, most of the players are employees at the works who train on average twice a week at night. Their spirit and dedication is second to none, yet by no stretch of the imagination should they have run Wigan to a last-minute winning try and in 1978 fail to topple Castleford by only one point in a 22-23 defeat. Amateur rugby produces the honest grafter, the player who is willing to run all day, but a player who, in the past, would have floundered against the greater experience, ability and, above all, size of the professsionals. Not so today, for such teams can approach the professionals with high hopes of success. It is in the forwards where the six-tackle rule has created the problems, increasing the amateurs' chances of victory.

Prior to its adoption in 1966, a League forward had to average fifteen or sixteen stones, and some like John Barton (Wigan) scaled in at eighteen stones. We needed this bulk to absorb the punishment in the head-on tackling which was a feature of the game, as packs grappled with each other for mastery in mid-field. A pack would 'soften up' its opposite set of forwards in the first fifteen minutes by suddenly launching a series of drives down the middle, often with fearless runners moving at pace on to some finely timed passes. When Brian McTigue and Frank Collier were sending out passes for John Barton, Roy Evans and Geoff Lyon in the Wigan pack, we at St. Helens had to absorb the punishment. A fifteen-stone body came at you at full pace from ten yards away, not with the intention of running round you but through you. Whether this is relished by the purist or not, the Northerner liked to see big men tackling each other aggressively. We may wince, but it was a test of manhood for both player and spectator. Therefore when a pack was tired, when it had taken its battering, few of its members were found standing out in the threequarter-line, few were able to detach themselves from midfield for the sole purpose of covering. We did not know where the next thrust would come from.

Today, the six-tackle rule has replaced the majority of the big men with lighter players, particularly in the second-row and loose-forward positions, who at times are faster than the backs. We now see ex-centres in the second-row, or ex-full-backs such as Kel Coslett (St. Helens and Rochdale) or Harry Pinner (St. Helens and England Under-24) in the loose-forward position, when they stand barely six foot in height. They are all excellent players in the present game, but most of these forwards lie flat and wide across the field, with the resultant disruption to any back play. The teams now line up as if they were in a Rugby Union Sevens formation with a sweeper behind. The ball is passed flat across the pitch from back to forward, from forward to back, without progressing upfield. This is highly interesting to the casual television viewer but hardly to the fan on the terraces. It is obvious that where, in Union, a side can pull its opponents' pack together at a maul or a ruck and clear the decks for the launching of their backs, this is not so now in League. The League side cannot afford to use up too many of its tackles in bringing the opponents' forwards, usually tired and spent, to the midfield. The build-up to achieve positions from which to launch back play cannot be done and so the play tends to become instantaneous and individualistic.

Apart from the adoption by Union of several of League's laws, the most basic change which has brought the codes closer has been the League player's inability to retain the ball for long stretches. Still not at that stage of the Union game where the player has to release the ball in the tackle (though he can absorb tackles in a maul by setting up second- and third-phase attacks), some similarities of positional play have begun to creep into both games. Yet I would still say to the new ex-Union convert or the intending signing that

114

the only real similarity is the ball. I must confess that, having watched League in St. Helens for fifteen years prior to my signing, I felt that I would cope easily. How wrong I was. It was a strange experience in my early days as I battled to master a completely new approach and acquire different skills while abandoning many once needed for Union.

Although I acknowledge the total commitment of the international Union player who is involved in the fierce competition of merit tables and the John Player Cup, he will rarely achieve the total dedication and professional approach of the League player. The player whose life-style depends on winning pay will train for and approach his game that much harder than the amateur, and yet the ex-Union player often fits very smoothly into the profess-ional ranks. A more relaxed attitude to rugby is often brought to the League game by the Union man, which blends with the single-mindedness of a local League player. That St. Helens should win all four trophies—the Challenge Cup, League Championship, Lancashire League and Lanca-shire Cup—in one year in 1966 with a blend of Alec Murphy, Bill Sayer, Albert Halsall and Tommy Bishop, all hardened professionals, and John Mantle, Cliff Watson, Len Killeen, Tom Van Vollenhoven and myself, all ex-Union players, is indicative of this mixture. Achieving this mixture is a difficult process for few can really guarantee that a world-class Union player will be a success at the League game. Players of the undoubted calibre of Robin Thompson (ex-British Lion), Tommy Gentles (South Africa's captain) and Keith Jarrett (Wales) failed to maintain the standards they attained in the amateur game while players such as Cliff Watson (Dudley Kingswinford R.U.F.C.) rose to heights undreamed of in their Union days.

Rugby Union is far less demanding of a player in terms of individual skills—an area where the convert may be found wanting in League. The stress, particularly for a forward, lies in collective techniques as in a maul or a line-out. League has little collective play of this sort, the emphasis being on the skills of the individual. For a Union coach it is a compar-atively straightforward task to knit a pack into being good maulers of the ball, given the right aggressive attitude, by a series of progressive exercises and regular practice. In League it is more difficult to teach a forward to handle a ball, time his passes to the split second, encourage him to pass out of the tackle, or synchronize the timing of his running on to the short pass. These qualities tend to be instinctive and it is on the extent to which the convert possesses these attributes that his success will be determined. Not all of these skills will be developed, but given some of them the League player will soon settle into his role. Cliff Watson, one of the finest prop-forwards I ever played with in both codes, had two fingers missing from his right hand which meant that he could never be a slick passer or ball handler. But few ran on to a ball more strongly and those now retired and nursing bruised ribs will testify to his strength in the tackle. The other factor which will determine the success of a Union convert will be the attitude that the player brings to the game. Many rather selfishly take the fat cheque and then are only too glad to wave the game farewell after a season or two. Many clubs have had their fingers burned by such a player, and now tend to reward players by a system of payments at the end of each season—an arrangement which binds the player to the club and gives him every incentive to continue.

12
Comparing the Incomparable

Skill is the vital ingredient of success whichever code you play under. But different laws and tactical methods require different skills. An outstanding Union player will not necessarily be a great performer in League rugby unless he can change his whole style.

The recent change of the role of full-back in Union has really opened up the game for this position, and players of the calibre of Andy Irvine and J.P.R. Williams have to possess the skills expected of the average League full-back. Full-backs in League, being unable to kick direct to touch, have always had to develop an attacking instinct as well as maintaining a rock-like defence. Indeed, full-backs with the attacking flair of League internationals Martyn Ryan and Austin Rhodes could create havoc in opposing threequarter-lines and were the forerunners of all the link moves which are now so common in the Union game.

The modern Union full-back must be one of the cleverest and fastest footballers in the team and he can be the main attacking player. Irvine's speed and sidesteps, for example, were used to good effect on the 1977 British Lions' tour where he took advantage of any loose kick. The League full-back will rarely kick the ball. Having gained possession he must make full use of the six tackles available, as it is senseless to surrender the ball for territorial advantage when your side has no guarantee of regaining possession. Geoff Pimblett, the St. Helens R.L.F.C. captain and Lance Todd Trophy winner at Wembley in 1976, is a fine example of the attacking full-back who has made the easy transition from Lancashire Rugby Union. He still plays a similar game to his Union days. I have assumed the accepted virtue of solid tackling from a full-back in both codes but in League he will be faced with far more occasions than his counterpart in Union, for he does not have a back-row and covering stand-off as lines of defence in front of him. Admittedly today most League clubs use a scrum-half or as in the case of Leeds a centre, in the shape of John Holmes, as a sweeper. Standing between the full-back and the other eleven players he now covers the short tactical kick or initial break. This has relieved the full-back of some work as the ball is often cut off before reaching him.

The defence, too, by the threequarters in League is vital, particularly from the set-piece play of the scrums. Here, apart from the full-back, they are indeed the last line of defence. There is no rampaging wing-forward to harass their opponents' line, no No. 8 covering behind them. They cannot hide. If you cannot tackle you cannot play League successfully. The threequarters, from the set scrum, must lie up flat on their opposite numbers as in Union, the only difference being that the open-side wing will also lie up flat. In Union he will invariably lie some five to ten yards behind his centre to cover for the kick to touch or the high diagonal punt, but in League, where the kick from a scrum is rarely seen, he is crucial to the defence. The whole threequarter line will sweep into their opponents on an arc as a hand on a clock moving from a quarter-past to half-past nine. Their intention is to get into the opposition's line to block the movement of the ball to the wing. It is now common to see the wing almost on his man before the ball has reached the inside centre.

Variations in defence which are highly effective are crossovers between the inside-centre and stand-off, and between the wing and outside-centre—a tactic rarely seen in Union because of the addition of flankers as an attacking medium. Given a big, strong inside-centre, a team will employ him to fly straight at the stand-off from his outside, the unexpected side. He will endeavour to block and crash-tackle him while the defending stand-off will move across behind the tackler to take the inside-centre, if he does receive the ball. Possibly the finest exponent of this technique was Duggie Greenall, the ex-Great Britain and St. Helens centre, who, flying through the air like a hawk, would swoop unexpectedly on the stand-off and leave him for dead on the floor. Dentists did roaring trade when Duggie was in town. Mick Sullivan and Billy Boston as wingers also mastered the art of the switchover. They would come in fast for the outside-centre, leave the wing to cover, and smother any hope of the ball getting to their opposing wing. This tactic can be most disconcerting to an outside-centre who is likely to be hit by the equivalent of a brick wall from his outside at the very minute that he receives the ball. Whenever we played against Wigan the cry would go up, 'Watch Billy! Watch him! ' to any youngster playing centre who might not be aware of his presence, lurking and hovering ready to flatten him with perfect precision. He was League's answer to a Rocky Marciano uppercut. I have rarely seen this tactic employed in Union, though I have used it to good effect in a schoolboy side. Grant Batty, the chunky New Zealand wing, was one of the few to attempt it.

'But why is it that League players always seem to handle and pass a ball better than the Union players? ' many ask, as if seeking a magic formula. The answer lies not in the coaching, though, as in League, I would encourage a boy to pass a ball with his wrists, propelling the ball away from him with the fingers and not with the classic copy-book Union style of extended elbows, swivel of the hips, lean away and all that jargon. The answer lies on the emphasis given to running and handling in the game and at training. A boy has to pass under pressure and be able to take a pass with his opponents almost on top of him at every training session in League, whereas in Union the majority of sides still look upon the game as a kicking exercise punctuated by the odd pass. Few will learn the necessity of good handling in a coaching session where the emphasis is on high punts to the full-back, chip-balls back to the box, and second-phase attacks with the back-row. All these techniques do have a vital part to play in Union and it is unfair to compare them with the straight, direct running and crisp handling of a League threequarter, who is given greater scope to take a tackle without fear of losing the ball. Hence he need not always have at the back of his mind the kick as a defensive weapon, which tends to become an obsession the more it is used. It must be admitted that League has lacked the variety given by tactical kicking and it is pleasant to see it creeping back under the six-tackle law possibly to cause a revision of a side's defensive planning in the future. As yet I would say the League player lacks the accuracy of a Phil Bennett in this department.

The League half-backs, however, certainly lack nothing to their opposites in Union. I am afraid that the legendary 'King' Barry John would certainly have lost his crown at Workington or Whitehaven, while the style of play of England's former stand-offs, Martin Cooper and Alan Old, both kicking players, would not suit the League game. As in Union, the League half-backs are the key to success of any side owing to their complete involvement in both attack and defence. Most scrum-halves in the League game are pocket battleships who take a positive delight in knocking the big men down, often, because of their fiery temperaments, looking for trouble. It is as if they have to assert themselves on the field as a substitute for their lack of height. In the 'unlimited tackle' days the scrum-half and the stand-off were invariably the first men into the opposition, causing no end of trouble, none more than Alec Murphy (St. Helens), Tommy Bishop (St. Helens) and Reg Bowden (Widnes). Such men would take great pride in toppling a sixteen-stone forward as he hurtled downfield, particularly Alex who, to the amusement of the crowd, would often wag his finger at the player and back chat to him before carrying out the tackle. I well remember Tommy Bishop in a fierce battle at Wakefield in a Challenge Cup match when both he and I were confronted by Rocky Turner, their international loose-forward.

Tommy, all five foot, false teeth and shoulder pads, shrieked, 'Leave him, let him come.'

I did and a cross-butt throw from Tommy saw Rocky being taken off with a broken collar bone. Result—St. Helens through to the next round of the Cup.

The scrum-half must be tough even today where many now act as the 'sweeper' behind the line of defence, cutting off any break down the middle of the field. Apart from his tackling, he must be an instinctive footballer and above all possess speed.

The Union scrum-half's first priority is his service from the base of the scrum and line-out. Gareth Edwards (Wales), for example, was able to pass a ball thirty or forty yards giving his stand-off ample room to manoeuvre. Only rarely will he make a break himself, being content to act as a link, or feed to his back-row, whereas the League scrum-half, again on account of his ability to retain possession in the tackle, will try to do much more from the base at the expense of a fast service. Here, speed away from the pack to escape the clutches of a loose-forward is the priority, plus strength in the shoulders to resist the tackle. Again his first instinct is to attack. Even on his own line a League scrum-half must go forward for there is no relieving kick to touch up his sleeve when he has to make the ball bounce first. This attitude sharpens him mentally and in speed of foot, though few are as fast as Alec Murphy, who in a Lancashire Cup Final against Swinton, where I was packing at loose-forward, actually picked the ball from my feet, beat his man, and scored under the post from twenty yards out before I had lifted my head from the scrum.

The tendency to absorb and waste a tackle does, however, limit the service from the League scrum. I feel that greater emphasis on service to the backs would be welcome and enlarge the opportunities for the threequarters. A real eye-opener for me was one of Bob Prosser's (ex-Newport R.U.F.C.) first games for St. Helens against a New Zealand touring side when, coming from Union, he gave an immaculate service of over thirty yards to the Saints' stand-off Wilf Smith who, along with his threequarters, served up a treat of fast, direct running for the crowd. Sadly he went the way of most League scrum-halves by losing the art. Comparisons are worthless, but I am inclined to think that Gareth Edwards was considered the world's finest scrum-half not for his kicking, his passing and his tackling, but because of the extra dimension which he brought to his game in the shape of accepted League skills—his speed, his strength and his desire to run with the ball. What a fine League player he would have made.

The scrum-half's partner at stand-off must also be strong, for he is the first man, in League, to make contact with a roving loose-forward. But there is room too for the ghost-like qualities of men such as Castleford stand-offs Alan Hardisty and Bruce Burton. Both were blessed with the ability to turn up in the right place at the right time, and, as a Union man would follow his flankers, so they picked up many tries from closely following up a second-row's breaks. The Union stand-off will hope to take the ball away from opposing flankers by sidestepping outside or moving round his opposite number. But the League man will require a short, neat side-step either way, since the direct break inside, with no flankers, can be highly effective and straightens the line for his inside-centre coming alongside. He will also be in the mould of a typical Welsh stand-off, jinking, sidestepping and weaving in a confined space as he seeks to escape the vice-like grip of a 'spotting' set of backs opposite. Attack will also be uppermost in his mind, for again he is unable to kick defensively, nor will he wish to surrender possession too early, and so he must run or pass the ball to a better-placed colleague.

An indication of the difference between the two roles can be seen in a comparison of Alan Old's play in a 1977 Yorkshire game where he won the match with his penalty goals and that of Bill Francis who was acclaimed man of the match in a St. Helens v Leeds game. Old, on receiving thirty passes, kicked twenty-two, ran two and passed the ball six times. Francis, on receiving thirty passes, ran eight, passed twenty-one and kicked one. Here lies the difference in emphasis, yet each played a big part in his side's winning of the game. If we bear these statistics in mind it can easily be understood why tricky, sidestepping footballers such as Tom Brophy, Martin Regan and David Watkins, are signed from Union and not such players as Martin Cooper or Alan Old. The League stand-off must commit himself to the game much more than his Union colleague whose defensive weaknesses and inability to beat his man can be hidden by his flankers and his kicking boot. The loss or addition of flank-forwards is crucial to the roles of the half-backs in either game as they are to the approach and make-up of both packs.

'A bloody shambles! ' 'A chaotic heap! ' Such cries of derision are overheard in a Rugby Union clubhouse when the steward switches the television over to BBC2's Rugby League Floodlit Cup on a Tuesday evening.

'Look where the ball comes out! That hooker's not

binding. Look where the prop's feet are, he'd get destroyed in our game,' proclaims the local Union front-row, as he sips his ale in the warmth of the lounge bar.

While 'Our Eddie' in his commentary seeks to take the viewer's attention away from the untidy mess, it is difficult to disagree with his casual judgement. Eddie Waring himself, in one of his lighter moments, suggested a funnel be placed above the hookers to drop the ball down to the middle of the scrum, while the ex-Rugby League secretary, Bill Fallowfield, in more serious vein, even suggested the possibility of the referee putting the ball into the scrums. This is an intriguing idea, but I can guess the reaction of a home crowd when their side want the ball badly in the last minute and the referee's hand slips.

Scrummaging has been accepted as the blight of the League game for many years and the fact that referees all too frequently allow advantage or overlook an infringement in the hope of maintaining continuity of the game is not to be condoned. Mick Naughton, the League's foremost referee, admitted on television that he will always seek to maintain the flow of the game. That is a laudable statement, but only if infringements are penalized. Despite the League's insistence on tighter control at the scrums, too much pressure is put on a referee today to keep the game open and to avoid many long scrummage sessions for the sake of the television viewer. I often feel that a referee is marked on how many times the ball gets away from the scrums rather than correct application of the laws. One well-known referee, Dickie Thomas, many years ago used to come into our dressing-room before a match and insist: 'I'll have the ball in the scrum first time; otherwise it's a penalty.' This was a rather dogmatic approach but it made front-rows observe the laws.

There has been a considerable improvement in the last couple of seasons since the Rugby League insisted on the loose-forward remaining attached to the scrum and making the scrum-half retire behind his own pack with the loose-forward. This has caused less friction between scrum-halves and I would welcome this practice in Union where I feel that a scrum-half should be able to pass the ball freely from the base of the scrum without his opposing scrum-half lying on his back as he picks up the ball. Those hairline decisions over whether a scrum-half is off-side would cease to occur and help the flow of the match. Is it then that League men cannot scrummage? Are they not skilled or strong enough? The answer is a firm 'No'. But there are many reasons why the techniques, cohesion and control of a Union scrum can be admired at the expense of League's version.

In Union the scrummage is looked upon as a vital component of the game, providing a fascinating set-piece for the watcher and a trial of strength and technique for the player. In the League game, however, the whole emphasis of the play is away from the scrums. Scrummaging is seen as a necessary interference in the continuity of open play, where front-row forwards who might be good ball-handlers, runners and tacklers would only lastly be expected to prop. Only rarely would a forward be selected for his propping ability. A club director, ever conscious of the player who is thrilling the crowds with his running and ball skills, would only look to a player's scrummaging ability as a last feature of his game. In ten seasons of League, I never saw a scrummage machine, a team practising scrummaging or a scrum-half combining with a hooker in training. There was a total absence of work in this aspect of play and therefore skills developed by the front-row tended to be individual rather than collective. Even referees are pressured by endless directives from League headquarters, stressing the need for open play and the removal of long sessions of scrummaging. Is it any wonder that they allow petty infringements to pass and play the advantage law to its fullest extent in order to please their bosses? Yet only by a strict emphasis on the scrums, a purge if you like, will any improvement be achieved. But this would require a patient public.

The problem is that a Union crowd is invariably made up of ex-Union players who can appreciate the niceties of scrummaging, whereas the League spectators are not unlike a soccer crowd in having fewer ex-players and more casual observers. I have no doubt that they would soon become frustrated at the rigorous application of the whistle. Even if the emphasis on the scrummage was corrected, the different techniques in both games would still produce different types of scrum.

In Union the front-row is expected to bind tight, props' legs back and well apart, and drive forward in unison with the other back five at a given signal. Here the open-side forward might be lifting his opponent to give his hooker a better sight of the ball, while the tight-head prop might be lowering his opponent to spoil the strike.

In League the open-side prop is an extremely large man who stands upright, lifting his opponent if possible, again to give his hooker a clear sight of the ball, but it is with the the hooker's position that the crucial difference lies. In Union the hooker must have his feet in a scrummage position before the ball is put into the scrum. In League he must only be bound with his arms, and consequently most hookers have their full bodies bent almost facing the tunnel with their legs as near as possible to the opening. With his open-side prop also attempting to split opposing prop and hooker, as soon as the ball is thrown by the scrum-half, he will thrust his whole body across the tunnel. In so doing he hopes to block his opposite number by smothering the opening so that the ball comes on to his legs or body, not just his foot as in Union. Guiding the ball back, at times almost with his whole body in a twisting movement, he will expect his open-side prop to pick up the deflection with his leg and help steer the ball. In practice, most balls are deflected back off the prop's feet into the glad hands of the scrum-half who is frequently waved 'play on' by the referee. In the words of Bob Dagnall, the ex-Great Britain hooker: 'If your scrum-half cannot pick up two out of three deflections from the tunnel, he is of little value to you.'

It is obvious then that with all the twisting and manoeuvring for position in the front-row the scrum is bound to lack stability and wheel or frequently collapse. It is here that the Union scrum has another tremendous advantage, in having wing-forwards or flankers. The flankers, by a low drive and packing at an angle, give stability to a scrum and concentrate all the push to the centre—it is only when the flankers are withdrawn from the scrum that the Union version can often look ragged. The abilities of the hooker in League are such a personal matter that if emphasis were given to correct binding and foot placing by the second-row and loose-forward I doubt whether it would make much difference. Hence most League back-three players approach the scrums, not as a rest, but with less conviction than they would approach a 'play the ball' situation. Though the entertainer Max Boyce in song lauds the legendary 'Pontypool front-row' of Price, Windsor and Faulkner, they would probably be less effective outside the Union game, while a front-row of Watson, Dagnall and Mills not only meets the requirements of League but would certainly lack nothing if forced to play under Union laws. Just as Union prunes the League game of its better laws, League surely misses a golden opportunity in not applying the rules similar to Union's at the scrums. I think the sad factor is that whereas the majority of the law-makers have played Union so few members of the Rugby League Council have ever played either game.

The Union forward must be considered primarily a 'ball winner' when presented with an endless supply of scrums, line-outs, rucks and mauls, but the League forward's role as a ball winner must be a secondary one as it is only at the scrummage that he actually seeks to win the ball for his backs. His primary function is as a 'ball user'. The Union player, therefore, will, from his early rugby days, develop certain techniques such as mauling which he will develop as part of his game. Sadly this is at the expense of many other skills I like to see in a forward. By a series of coaching ploys, he is encouraged to follow the ball round the field, his coach emphasizing the need to hunt as a pack and to arrive within seconds of a player being tackled. Such a Union pack might set up a maul or ruck with great skill without three or four forwards involved actually touching the ball. In contrast, the League forward does not follow the ball in his role of 'ball user', but, apart from the obvious backing up of a colleague or when working a set move, lies in space for the ball to come to him as he takes a pass from his stand-off or centre. In my early League games with St. Helens, I chased all over the field following play but never seemed to touch the ball until told by Bob Dagnall, our hooker, to 'slow thi'self down, lad, let it come to thee.' The ball had been sailing past me to forwards driving deep down the middle of the field, looking for gaps in the opposition. Hence different skills are created for both codes.

Props of the calibre of Ian McLaughlin and Sandy Carmichael (Scotland), or second-rows with the line-out skills of Nigel Horton (England) and Alan Martin (Wales), are seemingly lost in open play with its demands on running and passing. Rarely would a Union front-five man possess the handling skills or speed of thought of his opposites in League. Rarely would they stride down the middle of the field as would Phil Cookson (Leeds) and Phil Lowe (Hull K.R.) or have the speed and swerve of Eddie Cunningham (St. Helens) who has international honours for centre as well. And yet from my own experience, I do not think exciting ball-playing and running forwards such as John Tembey and Dick Huddart would have relished the donkey work of mauls and rucks in Union. The best examples of the different roles and the resultant creation of different skills was seen in the crucial County Championship match between Lancashire and Yorkshire in 1977. Billy Beaumont and Fran Cotton, two Lancashire and British Lions' forwards, are two of the best forwards in the world of Union and both, to me, have the qualities that would have stamped them as fine League players. In this match, despite their excellent performances, Cotton touched the ball twice when running and Beaumont three times. Compare this to a St. Helens v Leeds game where George Nicholls, the Great Britain second-row, handled twenty-three times when running. Here lies the difference in demands. A member of the front-five in a Union pack can play well without touching the ball with his hands; a League player must touch the ball to be in the game. It is only in the area of the back-row where these League skills are cultivated as a flanker links with his half-backs, as a No. 8 picks up from the base of the scrum, or as all three drive from a line-out peel. Any comparison, therefore, between forwards of the two codes is difficult and it is in the area of open play where the League scout will look for his possible convert. The scout would take a Union forward's tight play for granted, would look keenly at his handling, but would pay closest attention to his hardness and tackling.

If I was to tell Billy Beaumont that he made only four tackles in the same game or Fran Cotton that he made three, both would no doubt stare incredulously at me. But this is fact, for by tackles I do not mean all the mauling, shoving, pushing and weighting down of the ball which happens round a Union set-piece situation, but the incident of one man tackling another in the act of running with the ball. The Union forward's role in this respect is slight because all of the front-five forwards will be heavily involved in the hard, wearing-down process at maul, ruck and line-out. Rarely will they meet a man running full at them. Even the Union back-row will only take a front tackle when the opposing half-backs bring flankers or centres or crash balls back to the scrum. Most of their work will be in movement across the field which will result in the side tackle or the tackle from behind. The R.F.U.'s own coaching manual readily admits that, 'When the attacker is running hard, straight at the defender, this is possibly the most difficult tackle to perform.'

Once again we come to one of the basic differences in the two codes. With two sides flat across the field, as in League, the tackle from the front is inevitably the major one to come to grips with. Because there are no mauls, rucks or line-outs, the average League forward will be expected to make about thirty per match. This is where his energy will be sapped, not only in his tackling but in being tackled. The first thing I realized as a St. Helens R.L. player was that I could not shirk tackles. My tackling ability was always on view to the spectators, for with a flat defence anyone leaving a gap is easily seen and shown to be wanting. When a forward of some sixteen stones takes a ball from ten to fifteen yards away and builds up speed, he can take some stopping if the defender is only a couple of yards from the line. But the player will be all the more alert and aggressive when he knows that he is the only line of defence with all eyes on him. This situation frequently occurs in League and a forward must have the stamina to soak up the punishment. This aspect of the game suited me admirably because I loved to tackle. In League, with the set pattern from 'play the ball', a player knows who is coming to take him and therefore both are primed as two fighting cocks, each determined to outdo the other. I used to relish looking into the player's eyes, often shouting at him to come at me, talking to him when I had endowed him with a feeling of power. The ability to stand up over your victim and await the next 'play the ball' adds to this feeling of triumph after a good tackle.

Continuous front tackling is what makes the League game much harder than Union. We are not soft because we wear shoulder pads, we need them to absorb the bone-crunching thighs of a Boston or a Nicholls. Very often, particularly in 'unlimited-tackle' days, I have sat in a warm salt-soaked bath at Widnes or St. Helens on a Sunday morning, allowing my body to recover and tone up, looking at the black bruises standing out on my skin. Without those pads I shudder to think what my condition might have been. In this aspect of the game, the advice of the Rugby Union coaching manual is not of much value to the convert. The aim of the tackler is to stop the League forward from parting with the ball in the tackle. Therefore, if he tackles 'waist high, trying to knock him backwards' as directed, although useful on many occasions, the opponent might well be able to take the tackle only to slip a pass to another strong forward running at speed. Consequently the tackler must learn to be almost upright in the tackle and smother the runner so that he takes man and ball at the same time, therefore stopping any pass being made. In Union the man would resist the tackle and try to turn the ball back to a maul or roll away from it when on the ground to await the ruck. In both instances the movement has at least been stopped.

Forwards are not necessarily adept at both games for their roles are so widely different. Even in the Union game the play of a tight-head prop is worlds apart from that of an open-side flanker. Players in a Union pack can possess different skills, attributes and temperaments and yet be members of a common unit. In League both the prop and the loose-forward must be able to run, pass and tackle as well as being the possessors of sound footballing brains. All their skills must be somewhat similar since all their roles as individuals are closer together. Though both games differ to such a marked extent, the enjoyment and interest to be gained from playing both is similar on the field—a personal satisfaction in one's ability and fitness as well as a collective satisfaction in the team's success. It is in coaching and organizing the game, particularly at schoolboy level, that other benefits are also gained. Indeed, it is in coaching schoolboys that I have enjoyed the best of all possible worlds of rugby, my kind of rugby, playing and coaching for two different codes of the same great game.

13
The Young Ideal

For me, giving up the game was not an end, but a new beginning. I had always put my whole heart into playing rugby. And when I tried to pass on that commitment and enjoyment by coaching the young to fulfill their potential, I was doubly rewarded. It had been a pleasure to reach the top. But it was even more satisfying to coach others to reach the heights of which they were capable, or indeed just to play well enough to enjoy the game. On my retirement from Rugby League at Widnes, I was not faced, as many ex-players are, with suddenly having a vacuum in my life. I had been enjoying coaching rugby—both Union and League—for many years while I was still playing. Little did I know, however, that this would give me more pleasure and even greater excitement than actually being involved in a match. I feel the reason for this is that, as a schoolmaster, the bulk of my work has been done with schoolboys. Irrespective of which code they are playing, it is very satisfying to see their skills developing and this is often more rewarding than working with adults.

In Rugby League, a first-team coach at a club such as St. Helens, Widnes or Leeds need pay little attention to the development of individual skills for, as professionals, the majority already possess the skills on arrival at the club. As such, the major concern of the coach must be, apart from fitness work, the blending and welding together of the individuals into a team. Attention must be given to planned moves, tactics and styles of play to suit different teams, competitors, or even grounds. While the satisfactions to be gained from developing a Cup-winning unit for Wembley or a championship are obvious, the pleasure to be derived from seeing the development of a player as an individual in club rugby is not as strong. Nor are the personal relationships forged as close and satisfying as the schoolmaster with his players, first as boys, later as men.

During my time as 'the Invisible Man' or coach to St. Helens R.U.F.C., I had a vast array of young talented players, all eager to learn the requirements of club rugby. The great majority already possessed the natural skills fostered at school, which enabled them to move to the highest levels of club and county Rugby Union, one or two even playing for their country. Players of this calibre were destined to stride to the top and only needed a certain emphasis in their coaching. My main problem during those years was time, for, despite the natural skills of the St. Helens players, they were not physically or mentally mature enough for our strong Northern fixture list. So, during defeat, I had to stress the value of discipline both on and off the field which would be necessary for eventual success. An atmosphere and professional approach had to be given to the club, a disciplined environment had to be created, while such players were given time to develop over a period of three or four seasons. Therefore a certain style of play had to be developed which would hide their youth and inexperience and yet at the same time help their undoubted skills to flourish.

Living in St. Helens and with their League background, many had an advantage in being able to blend the unit skills of Union with the individual skills of League. Coaching in Union must never produce a side which is ruled by tight play and set ploys. The coach must always strive to create the side which, given the right grounding in all the basic techniques, will produce running football. He must never kill the desires of a player to express himself as an individual on the field. Nowhere is this blend of League and Union more vital than in the area of forward play, though I would be the last person to advocate a decline in the traditional sessions which drill a Union pack into an efficient outfit. I would advocate a grafting on of League attitudes for the Union forward as an extra in his training routines. A coach must have a solid platform from which to launch his running play and he must obviously give much time to his pack, working on scrummage machines to ensure correct foot positions, correct binding and a low drive. He must indulge in the countless exercises designed to increase the pack's proficiency at mauling and rucking a ball.

He must spend endless hours throwing a ball in at the line-out where techniques for securing possession can be developed. Such application will produce what I have suggested earlier is the distinctive feature about a Union pack, a complete unit of eight men.

Given the required size of forwards, with the right aggressive instincts, a coach should be able to create a highly efficient body of ball-winners. A coach whose work I admired was John Burgess (the ex-England coach) who brought such an attitude to my own county, Lancashire, where, despite all the running skills to be found, they had rarely produced forward dominance to match that of counties such as Warwickshire and Gloucestershire. He stressed the importance of this base before allowing the traditional Lancashire back-play to flourish. There is a belief among players and spectators that if a prop cannot sidestep, swerve, or dummy then he is not doing his job. The fact that he can scrummage an opponent into the ground is often regarded as of little consequence. Therefore Burgess's job was to bring players with a League attitude, like mine at St. Helens, back to the bread-and-butter approach to Union forward-play, and he provided the basis for later coaches to win the County Championship.

The problem with English Rugby Union in the seventies is that there are not these two layers of skills and the emphasis, particularly in the South and South-West, seems to be on the unit skills to the detriment of all else. Coaches should concentrate on both aspects of forward-play in their sessions. Just as in the concept of 'total football' in soccer, where defenders become attackers and vice versa, so we should look at 'total rugby' where forwards can perform as backs as well. Emphasis must be placed upon their speed, even that of prop-forwards, and in particular their handling and passing of the ball. I would advocate at least a session once a fortnight where forwards do nothing but handle the ball and I would recommend that they indulge in many hours of touch rugby alongside backs and are not hived off to some other part of the field as inferior specimens.

Though such handling and passing skills must be dealt with at an early age at school when a boy is eleven or twelve, it is never too late to try to graft on what is missing. A forward, apart from his weekly training-sessions, will scrummage or jump at a line-out some forty or fifty times a game where he will gain all the experience necessary, but in the Union game he may only have the ball in a running position some half a dozen times. Many would argue that this proves where the emphasis in coaching must lie. I would maintain, however, that those six occasions in which he handles the ball will be vital in the scoring of tries. The forward's ability to give an accurate pass, draw the opposition on to himself, or give a dummy pass can be the crucial turning point in the eighty minutes of a game. It can be the difference between winning and losing, which the vast majority of scrums and line-outs are not. There is no worse sight in Union than to see the forward who suddenly finds himself in clear space on a field and does not know what to do, or the forward who, given a scoring opportunity, ruins it through his inability to draw an opponent and time his pass to a colleague. Touch rugby, with many players to a side, will create the need to avoid players, to beat a man with an accurate pass, and to learn to take a pass under great pressure. All forwards should try to possess these abilities.

One of the finest back-rows for England since the war was surely that of Peter Robbins, Alan Ashcroft and Reg Higgins (interestingly the son of an ex-Rugby League international) who, though possessing all the graft and tackling powers necessary to cope with any opposition, displayed that extra layer of rugby skills. Their play at the base of a scrum opened up many a defence with their close passing, while their skill at picking up a loose ball after a tackle and developing a movement among the backs allowed full scope for running rugby. Rarely was one of this back-row at a loss as to what to do with the ball when he was given a gap on the field. Alan Ashcroft has often voiced a theory, and I would subscribe to it, that the trend in the seventies of playing huge back-rows in order to secure line-out possession at all costs, has been disastrous to the arts of back-row play. He contends that many players, when over 6 ft. 3 in. tall, lose the agility and ability necessary to bend and keep low to the ground when scooping balls from the base of the scrum to indulge

in close inter-passing under the greatest of pressure. The rise
to prominence of the England pack in the seventies has been
due to players who had this extra layer of rugby ability
and who learned their rugby in the Lancashire club or
schools' environment. British Lions such as Billy Beaumont
(Ellesmere College), Fran Cotton (Newton Le Willows G.S.),
Tony Neary (De La Salle G.S., Salford) and Roger Uttley
(Blackpool G.S.) can add a further dimension to their game.
Outraged Southern purists should please note four England
captains here.

The natural instinct for a person when confronted with
a round ball is to kick it, but surely the natural instinct for
the oval ball, which fits lovingly and snugly into the hands, is
to pass or run with it. All players must be encouraged to
develop this desire though, even more sadly, in recent years
many of our backs in Union appear to have lost it. I would
lay the blame on the too rigid and undue emphasis on coaching and tactics by the Rugby Football Union's coaching
system. In recent years we have become too obsessed with
the qualifications of the coach as he jogs round the field in
his badge-bedecked tracksuit, his clip-board in his hand,
barking out instructions to players about to embark on a
3,000-metre run to test recovery rates in fitness. He ponders
to recommend an aerobic or an anaerobic system of training
for his players. Have we all gone mad? Are we training for
the Olympics or for Rugby?

We have created a hierarchy of coaching panels from those
considered to have passed a sufficient number of examin-
ations to take the international players, through those capable of taking county teams, down to those capable of taking
the club team, with the majority rigidly adhering to the
leaflets, pamphlets and diagrams necessary to create the complete team. There are, however, many who, despite being
within this intricate framework, such as Mike Davis and Terry
Fallon of the English Schools' sides, have never stuck rigidly
to the dogma and have developed sides of real flair. There
have even been many national coaches I would not have put
in charge of my Under-12s' 'B' team. Alternatively, I can
think of many men without the badges who would be more
than capable of taking the England team.

Coaching is vital to the welfare of rugby, but we could do without the regimentation of recent years which has produced automatons instead of players. As coaches, we must give the game back to the players and not treat them as slaves to the coach's ideas. We must develop our backs first as individuals and second as a unit, not vice versa as I see so often. With many coaches at club level the norm has been the production of an endless supply of 'crash ball centres' where all centre-threequarters are taught how to make a short pass and crash back towards the pack in order to set up another endless round of mauling or rucking for the ball. We have produced the same type of back throughout the country and when it is necessary to coach such players at club level we are too late. The talents and attitudes to be developed for good back-play must be nurtured within the schools when the players are young and receptive to new ideas. The youngster must not be filled with the watered-down version of the handed-down coaching manuals, for such material should be used sparingly, and he must not become indoctrinated with a slavish adherence to a coaching programme. He must be given freedom to run wherever he desires. The tightening up of the nuts and bolts of his game can be done in his later years at school.

I am often amused at the eulogies of praise heaped on a coach who is supposed to have 'made' the latest superstar. Whenever I read of the tricks to teach the sidestep or the swerve I can only smile, for such skills are not taught: players are born with the skills. Barry John and Phil Bennett in Union and Alec Murphy and Billy Boston in League were not taught their tricks. They were born with them. Such men were gifted and instinctive players as youngsters who only needed the correct attitude, discipline and environment to succeed. I can point to many youngsters who, as eleven-year-olds in a school side, are equally as blessed in a repertoire of skills. The prime factors as to whether they succeed are the atmosphere in which they are placed and the will to succeed of the boys themselves. The secret lies in those schools where the attitudes and atmosphere generated by the coach can raise the ordinary back to international standard. It is necessary to let the boy's talents flourish and not be stifled by too many set drills. Many schools produce fine teams year after year, but produce few players who move on to heights of excellence on leaving the school. Here mediocre players are raised to higher levels of performance by a rigid adherence to planned drills at the expense of the gifted and natural player. Those schools which have regularly produced a supply of international backs have found the right balance where backs have been given the chance to realize their flair without fear of incurring the coach's wrath by ruining his set ploys.

If we are to instil in players the drive to run with the ball, we must look to the eleven-year-old in the schools or the junior in the club's mini-rugby sessions to produce what Rugby Union wants most. Again, we must encourage players in the accepted League virtues of crisp handling, slick passing and inventiveness if we are to produce again what for me was the finest touring side of the last twenty years, the Lions of 1974 in South Africa. Here the Irishman Syd Millar achieved a perfect blend of pack power and technique allied to craft and inventiveness in the backs, which produced ten tries in winning the four-match series. It was a pleasure to see grafting forwards taking part in sweeping passing movements and observe backs who could score for themselves without recourse to the set move, as in American football. They were coached, they were drilled, but they were given individual freedom within the unit disciplines.

It is with these attitudes in our minds that I and the rugby staff at Cowley School approach our junior teams and in particular our eleven-year-old intake. After the school's first-team, they must be the most important side in the school and must receive first-class attention from a master-in-charge. It is suicidal for a school to assume that an Under-12s' team can be left to any member of staff who might have a passing interest in rugby or be given to an older member who is merely being put out to grass. These new players are at the most impressionable age and will acquire attitudes and skills which will never desert them—they need a top coach. In this respect, I am extremely lucky to have a man as capable as Brian Middlehurst who looks after our side and gives them their grounding in running football. From the day of their

first games period, all the boys are divided into groups of
twelve. They are not told any laws save that they cannot
pass a ball forward and are told to run at each other or round
each other. With a teacher in the middle who can throw a
ball to any boy on either side, they can immediately begin to
enjoy the game and are suddenly made aware of the satisfaction in making physical contact in the tackles. The two
sides of six players usually play in a twenty-five-yard square
so that there is no room for any boy to hide. All the
players can be brought into the game at any time by the
master who controls the ball from the centre and who can
pass it to anyone when on the run. This should continue for
about half a dozen sessions, for the boys will relish running
with a ball and all will seek to score tries. Give them a sense
of competition, urge them to beat the other side and give
them every encouragement for winning. Please do not subscribe to the current attitude that playing is the thing. Of
course it is, but the best players are only those who will
strain to win. You will achieve nothing with the mentality
that treats the games period as a time for fresh air and an
afternoon out.

At Cowley School we rarely indulge in the many exercises
which are designed to work in groups of three or four players
running up and down a field or round in circles practising
passing. We never have groups of boys sitting on the grass
listening to long and boring lectures on the laws of the game.
We play, play and play at all times. Though the first weeks
may be chaotic, and the games only faintly resemble Rugby
Union, nevertheless a form will emerge as the laws are explained during play and as players are penalized for infringements. They learn to pass, to beat men, to try things on
their own in situations where they have to and not for the
sake of a practice move. Players of talent, class and with the
right aggressive tendencies will begin to show through. Here
again, unlike many schools, I believe in playing matches and
more matches. Therefore, where some only play two or three
matches in the first year in the belief that their boys are still
learning the game, we play twenty-five matches in the belief
that a boy will only learn the game under testing competitive
conditions.

Our first match usually takes place within a fortnight of starting school. Bear in mind, though, that Brian Middlehurst has probably had the boys out at every lunch hour and evening for fourteen days. They will enjoy it as they see something positive in sight. Even greater enjoyment will come from the direction not to kick the ball under any circumstances when playing for the team. Even though their position may be critical at times, the necessity to run will eventually become a desire to run by the time they are fifteen when the other techniques of the game and the necessity to kick can be grafted on. Nor is his attitude and application on the field the only thing of importance; the atmosphere off the field within the school must be equally absorbing for the boy. His attention must be diverted to rugby through colourful displays on the notice boards, frequent trips to top matches and fund-raising ventures to send him on tours throughout the country. His parents too must become part of it all by attending the socials and functions for rugby funds.

For the keen youngster there will be a real sense of purpose to his dedication and efforts; such will be the attachment to his school and its teams that he will become a player with ability, and more important, one with pride, that vital factor. Without this he will win nothing.